Smile Again

By Kim Gemmell

Smile Again

ISBN: 978-1-62249-568-9

Published by
Biblio Publishing
Columbus, Ohio
BiblioPublishing.com

Smile Again is an enlightening, motivational book about anecdotes and manifestations to live our best life. Whether we are going through a challenging time, or are seeking some positive enhancements in our life, it will provide inspiration and thought-provoking revival.

The first few chapters contain a recap of my first book in order to explain what enabled me to provide people with ideas and support to live our best life.

The following chapters talk in detail about great life lessons learnt through my experience, and interesting insights for general personal growth.

Whether we are going through great adversity, or simply enjoy helpful encouragement and inspiration, **Smile Again** will provide an easy, inspiring and entertaining read.

Smile Again

Smile Again

Forward

FINALLY!

Well I figured this is as good time as any to write my second book. Being in self-isolation because of our current pandemic with Covid-19 gives many of us the opportunity to get some things crossed off our list. And that's all what this book is about... finding the positives in challenging times of great adversity.

You'll find that is pretty much the common denominator in all my chapters. Mostly various anecdotes to break through barriers, tools to step outside of the box and reach a sustainable continuity of happiness, fulfillment and joy; even following dark days.

Keep the Faith, Hope and Love.   April 7, 2020

We are enduring a catastrophic time... people are sick and many dying all over the world. We are fighting an invisible enemy and parts of the world are getting bombarded. It's a very surreal and unpredictable time. We don't know when it will end or how many will be in the wake of its toll. We are all affected and cope in different ways. Some will go into depression or high anxiety; some will step up to help their vulnerable neighbor and friends, or keep busy doing things - like spring cleaning and getting in better shape. The number of couch potatoes will likely multiply. There are countless effects, but there is one common denominator that we all share. How we decide to proceed during bad times is a very important choice which will determine our outcome, and likely affect those who we live with or have relationships with.

People will pass blame for their actions and behaviors, but when you point a finger at someone else, you have three pointing back at you. Take accountability for your actions. I see people on social media ranting and raving, complaining, hating and shaming. What good does that do? It just spreads more doom and negativity.

I also see people finding some positivity and helping others. People making masks and donating them, people checking in on those who are alone, or vulnerable. Cheering on and praising all our frontline workers and heroes. We all can help and serve in some way, even if it is following the rules by safe distancing, or just staying home, we all can make a difference.

My daughter Jesse, who is autistic, is not going to her daily program because it is closed. Yet she is stepping up to help me every day with house and yard work, doing crafts and making necklaces and selling by donation, so she can give to the charities she works for. She has been a huge support providing encouragement to her other special needs friends who are feeling scared. Although she has struggled with anxiety in the past, she is making the best of it and is being as productive as she can.

We hold the power to win over evil. We have a choice with what we do and say. We must lift people up, come together, and think before we judge. We are the illustrators to our children who set the example, and we all want to be great role models for our children. Let's take the lead, not just during this pandemic, but whenever we are faced with adversity. This is our wake-up call.

I've started gathering some feedback from people to find out what positive things have come from living through this crisis so far and will share some of them once they've been collected.

I am enlightened and emotionally moved from various perspectives. I'm not sure where the world will be when my book is finished. And I don't know when I will have the book finished, but we will continue to find the silver linings.

For those who lose loved ones from this dreadful virus, I give my sincerest condolences. Losing loved ones are the worst times for us to bear, and so much more heart-wrenching in the wake of this pandemic. I pray for healing and strength for you all.

For the frontline workers risking their life every day to save others, you are truly our heroes. Your selflessness is noble, and once this dreadful virus is behind us, we will celebrate and honor you in the way you deserve. For now, we will follow the rules, keep practicing the safety measures, and do all we can to help lessen the burden for you.

Sometimes powerful lessons come from great peril. When tragedy struck my own life, I couldn't see a light at the end of the tunnel, and I didn't think I ever would. But sometimes adversity leaves a gift. An opportunity to live a more flourished life and engineer a change of destiny.

When my son Avery was born, he spent his first five months living in the hospital with a critical heart defect and many days where he was not expected to live. I experienced one of the most devastating experiences a human can be faced with. I would give up my own life for my children. We all would. However, this experience gave me a purpose to give back, and support all I can who will experience their own crisis or be affected with the challenging times like we are currently experiencing. Through my plight I was able to discover a purpose and turn my 'wounds into wisdom'. Having the time now, as well as knowing our nation will find fortitude from its perspective, I felt the need to get started now.

Smile Again

6

Chapter One
Bravery

"I love those who can smile in trouble, who can gather strength from distress, and grow brave by reflection."

~ Leonardo da Vinci

My first book, *Bravery; Our Journey of Faith, Hope & Love*, was about our family's journey following Avery's heart defect. I was inspired to write this memoir because the experience became a catalyst for a change of fate. Sometimes when we look back on life, we can see the steps on the path that lead us to where we are, and all the fortitude and wisdom we learned along the way. The people, the mentors, the chance encounters that became our guides.

I was very fortunate to grow up with wonderful loving parents. Along with my younger brother, Steven, we lived on a little hobby farm. I had my own horse at five years old. I couldn't ride it by myself so my dad would lead me around the farm for the first six months. My friends thought I was spoiled, but I appreciated every little thing my parents gave me, and never took anything for granted.

My dad did not have a good family life and grew up very poor. His dad left at an early age and his mom was not at all loving or supportive. He left home at 15 years old and worked very hard to have all he achieved. Perhaps that's why he was so generous with us kids. In his late teens and early adulthood, he became a professional boxer, and later became a gravel truck driver and purchased his own business. He worked a lot but would always have time for my brother and me. He was an Irishman with a feisty temper, but the most loving father, husband and friend. He was a very kind, generous man who literally gave the shirt off his back and his lunches away to the hungry.

My mom was a beauty queen, and just as beautiful on the inside with a sincere kind and positive demeanor. She was a dedicated mom that came on all our field trips and always putting ourselves before her own. Almost every weekend was taken up either at soccer tournaments or horse shows. Back then I never realized her sacrifice of time for me. She was a softy, which was a good balance to my dad. But I had strict rules which instilled very good values, manners and respect.

I still remember my first day of Kindergarten, and the enormous fear to go inside the school.

I said, 'I can't do it Mom." She said, "Honey, there is no such word as can't. I'm not going anywhere and will stay for however long you want me to." I don't know why that memory stuck with me so well over all these years. Maybe it was because it was my first lesson on how to face my fears, and what a wonderful mom I had.

Not only did I have the most supportive parents who filled my life with unconditional love, I also had my grandma next door. Growing up, I spent most weekends on her farm and unbeknownst to us, she blessed me with the outlook on life that would determine a mighty strength I would need in my adulthood. Grandma had only one leg because in her thirties, two cars drag racing smashed into each other and her. They couldn't even find her until the police spotted a tiny piece of her colorful dress. After she was pulled from the wreckage she called out for my mom, who was 14 and had witnessed it all from their car. She said, "Barbie, I'm not going to leave you," then slipped into unconsciousness as the ambulance took her away.

Later that day, the family was called in to say their good-byes because her right leg was crushed, and she was bleeding out. But a miracle happened when a blood clot formed to stop the bleeding. Unfortunately, though, her leg was crushed beyond repair and needed to be amputated.

This never slowed Grandma down and, in fact, she would go on to live the most self-serving life I know. She would visit anyone in Chilliwack who had a serious accident to help them by cooking for them and running errands. She'd take them to the best prosthetic places if they lost a limb. She was always baking bread to bring, along with other groceries, to those who were in need. I remember her baking birthday cakes and bringing presents for people who had no money.

She even took in a homeless man who couldn't take care of himself anymore and only spoke Swedish. He was her neighbor and lived in a tiny little run-down shack next door. When his health began to fail, she moved him into the spare room and took care of him for over 4 years until his passing.

When I was young, I remember thinking, 'why is Grandma so happy all the time, and always singing cheerful songs?' I'd wake up on most weekends to the smell of homemade waffles, or bacon and eggs. She would always sing, "Good morning Kimmy... It's another wonderful day!" Sometimes it would be raining, and I would think, what's so great about it. But when I was older, I got what she meant. She meant it was another day to spend alive and with the ones we loved.

I remember Grandma saying how she never thought to appreciate all the value and great things her legs did... like the simple act of walking or riding a bike. I grew up with great respect for her, but I never really knew the magnitude of wisdom she gave me until I needed to find the strength to endure my own crisis. If we are fortunate enough, we can learn, adapt, and find ways to make peace with adversity.

When I was twenty-one, I moved to Vancouver to attend BCIT, and ended up living there for quite a few years. Not long after I moved there, I was fortunate to meet my future kind and loving husband, Cam. We bought a cute little house and a few years later had our beautiful daughter Jesse. Life was cruising along just as good as I could have ever wanted or planned, and we were excited about the arrival of our second baby, oblivious to the oncoming storm. When people are not expecting something, I see why is equated to 'hitting a brick wall' because that's what it felt like.

Almost a month before my due date, excruciating pain sent me into the hospital. Within a minute of laying on the hospital bed I felt a huge gush of fluid. I thought my water must have broken but when I looked down, the white linens were soaked with blood. In seconds, I was whisked to the O.R. for an emergency C-section. When I became conscience, I was told I had delivered a baby boy, but the look on the nurse's face told me this wasn't the celebration it was supposed to be.

She said, "Hi honey, are you feeling okay?" I nodded. Then she said, "You have delivered a baby boy, and I am sorry dear, but he is very sick. He was born blue and not breathing. We resuscitated him and a team of specialists from Children's Hospital are on their way to get him. I'll go and get your husband now."

Just like that... in the blink of an eye, my life was forever changed. I didn't even hold Avery, and briefly saw him being taken away into the transfer ambulance. I couldn't see what he looked like because of all the machines hooked up to him, but I could tell he had a beautiful head of strawberry-auburn hair. I was too sick to be discharged and had lost a lot of blood. So, for two days, I laid in my hospital bed wondering if I'd ever get a chance to hold my baby alive. There is no other way to describe it - I was in a living hell.

What followed were many months of heart surgeries and setbacks, yet our little Avery wasn't giving up and continued to defy all the odds. Renal failure, respiratory arrests, and Code Blues were just a few of the obstacles Avery would have to overcome. So many times, the chances were against us, and one after the other, hopes to raise are only dashed with more and more setbacks.

I was Avery's mom, but I couldn't save him. Sitting beside him in the chair all day, watching the machine breathing for him, I felt invisible and helpless.

However, during our stay it was outstanding to see how all the surgeons, nurses and doctors rallied in desperation to save Avery, and fall in love with this tiny little guy who was determined to survive. Spending so many months in ICU became very taxing and I would try not to think about the stability of my mental health.

Not only were we facing the weight of everything Avery was going through, but all around us were very sick babies and children. Over time we became acquainted with many families, some of which babies did not survive. And some of who had the same defect as Avery — Transposition of the Great Arteries.

One of the families we got to know quite well spent many months beside us in ICU. Her name is Reena and her prognosis grave. I would look at her parents and see such broken faces, very sad eyes. I thought that is how Cam and I must look to others... kind of like we were only half alive.

Throughout our five months stay at the hospital we were bombarded with one hurdle after the other. Our beautiful little Jesse would receive a diagnosis of Autism, and the worst of all, the untimely passing of my beloved Dad. It was a Saturday morning on July 18th, and my Dad was at home alone while my mom was out with her friends at garage sales. Sometime in the hour my mom was gone, Dad suffered a massive heart attack and died at only 59. My world was shattered, no words could describe the despair.

Prior to this, I could feel in my heart that his health was deteriorating. He had high blood pressure and I feared all this was too much for him, I could see it in his eyes.

Up until then, I never asked, 'God, why me?' I just didn't know how I would cope with all this happening at the same time. I remember feeling I wanted to be in a coma because waking up every morning was more painful each day. We didn't even have time to grieve the loss of Dad because our lives were consumed with Avery's survival. But somehow, I knew Dad had traded his life for Avery's, and this brought me some comfort.

We had to go on, but with our hearts completely broken. For months I carried the fear and reality I may lose Avery too, and prayed for just one more day. I tried the best I could to remain positive, but it was hard when there was no escape from the suffering, and all around us was despair.

We would only leave Avery's side to get a bite to eat, or for a few hours' sleep in our RV in the parking lot. I can't even count how many times Cam and I would get calls in the middle of the night to come to ICU because Avery was crashing. But each time he would defy the odds and pull through. No one could believe his resiliency. Geez... I still remember hearing that phone ring like it was yesterday; my heart literally skipping a beat. When the phone rings in the middle of the night, you know it's not good news.

All these years later, I remember every detail, even the distilled smell in the air. Some days stand out more than others, particularly one where Avery was in day three of renal failure and the dialysis was not working. He hadn't much time left before the buildup of toxins would kill him. I can't begin to describe my pain and fear sitting there so powerless. Then an idea came to me and I ran to the hospital library and got on the computer. I looked up reflexology and found the foot chart where the kidneys were located. Then I ran back into ICU and began massaging his tiny little feet where the kidneys are located.

The doctors were making their rounds and stopped to ask me what I was doing. I said, "I'm using reflexology to stimulate Avery's kidneys to pee." They gave me a grin that looked either perplexed or hopeful. Avery did pee about 5 hours later.

We will never be certain if it was dialysis or the stimulation from reflexology, but I think I know, and it felt good to finally feel some purpose.

Occasionally we would find something to laugh about. Oh, it felt so good to laugh. For a spell I thought I had forgotten how until one day in the Mother's Room pumping my breast milk. Five times a day I would wander down the hall to pump my milk in the hopes that one day Avery would be off life support and able to drink it. I had gotten pretty good at using the enormous cow-like milking machine and could prop up the bottles to my knees and even read a magazine while the bottles filled. However, the first time I used it was not so pleasant. I didn't realize the suction was on high, and well.... let's just say I never thought my breasts would return to normal. Anyway, this time as I began to pump, I happened to look down to see my usual cream-colored milk had turned a bright neon green!

I thought, 'Oh no! My milk has gone bad. The stress of everything has finally gotten to me. Now I am completely useless and no good for anything!' I slowly headed back to ICU, covering my hands over the bottles as to not to disclose this alien colored milk. I sheepishly handed it over to the nurse who labels it with my name and then I put it in the fridge.

I said, almost in tears, "I'm afraid my milk has gone bad."

I was surprised to see her begin to grin... *This is so not funny. What is the matter with this lady? The only thing I can contribute to the aid of my son is now gone. How could you be so callous?*

Sensing my malaise, she quickly asked me what I ate for supper last night. With a bit of hesitation because I wasn't eating much these days, I said, "Uhm, pesto pasta."

"Honey..., That's why your milk is green. Nothing is wrong with your milk, other than perhaps its' garlic content. Under the circumstances you are a hero to keep producing during all the trauma you've endured." She proudly stated.

With the relief I laughed so hard, and that's when I realized it was the first time I smiled or laughed in probably two months. Every time I opened the freezer to place more bottles, I noticed the bright neon green fade and return to normal by the next morning. But I chuckled every time I opened the freezer as I thought what the other moms must be wondering when they looked at the bottles clearly labeled with my name. Who is this Kim Gemmell person with the bright green milk?

It was early in the second month of our hospital stay, and shortly after Dad died that a phenomenon occurred that helped me realize we are never alone when I began to find four-leaf clovers everywhere, even though I wasn't outside all that much. I knew they were signs from my grandma in Heaven because I would always find four-leaf clovers on her farm as a child, and she was bewildered with how many I would come across. Sometimes two or three in a day, and sometimes when I was riding through the field on my horse. The fact that I suddenly kept finding them again, especially not around much grass, told me this was no coincidence! It gave me strength during the many challenging months.

As the final surgery to cut off and switch Avery's Great Arteries approached, our fears elevated. This was a huge surgery and Avery barely survived the other three. It had to have been faith that kept me sane, I think. And thinking back on it all I found a truth:

You never know how strong you are, until being strong is your only choice...

Bob Marley

Thanks, Bob Marley.

I remember that early morning when I saw our surgeon walk into the surgical daycare ward about 6:00am to perform Avery's final surgery to fix his heart at last. He had an extra-large cup of coffee in his hands and all I could think was jeepers, I hope that is decaf! His huge hands had to operate on Avery's little tiny heart; the size of a walnut. The great arteries he had to cut off and switch were the size of a pin. One false move and that's it.... a certain fate of death.

Thankfully, as my Grandma did, Avery experienced his own miracle of survival when his fourth and last surgery to fix his heart was a success. Thanksgiving Day, October 10th, 1998 Avery was discharged to come home.

Because he was on life support for all those months, he was delayed; the size of a newborn at five months, and only seven pounds! Because of all he went through, the doctors believed he would likely have physical and mental setbacks. But I didn't care what kind of shape he was in; I got to bring him home when there were too many times, I didn't think I would.

Smile Again

Chapter Two
Fast Forward

"You'll find that life is still worthwhile if you just smile."
~ Charlie Chaplin

What I thought was the worst thing that could have ever happened to me back in 1998 was one of the best. Avery and Jesse are true blessings who fill my life with unconditional love, gratitude and joy!

Since birth, Avery continues to show his determined spirit and special abilities. Because of the lack of oxygen during his Code Blue, Avery was diagnosed with mild Cerebral Palsy and has a stiffer right hand and leg. It hinders his dexterity to a certain degree, but he doesn't let that get in the way. He has always refused to live with limitations, teaching me, and many others, the value of perseverance and resiliency. He never lets his disability define him... he defines his disability.

As he grew, I could see how his will and determination was not something he had to try to achieve... he was born with it, and his conviction gave him the strength to not only survive but thrive. However, he could do no wrong in our eyes, and got away with way too much! We were just so happy he survived, and because of all he went through, we often let him have his way.

I remember saying to Bonnie, (Avery's primary ICU nurse who became a wonderful family friend,) "Do these heart kids grow up to be spoiled brats?" And she said, "No, they actually grow up to be the most kind and gentlest souls." I remember hoping she was right.

No one had seen anything like him! Cam and I had to take turns watching Avery one on one, especially if we were going out somewhere. Short of swinging from the chandeliers, he was a going concern. Our house was locked up like Fort Knox in order to keep him from escaping. Even with that he managed to escape a couple of times. We found out years later that he twice got away from his Grandma Madge and Papa's house. Only they didn't tell us for fear we wouldn't let them babysit again!

Avery had so much energy and vitality, that I said to Dr. Human, Avery's cardiologist, at one of our follow up visits, "Did you put a bionic heart in this kid?" He laughed, "No, he's just making up for lost time."

At nine years old, Avery would be back at Children's Hospital for another surgery. However, this one was to cut and stretch out his Achilles tendon and cast for two months to provide more flexibility and coordination for walking. Most parents would probably be stressed out about surgery of any sort, but after four heart surgeries in five months, I was thinking ... 'Oh this will be a cake walk — we won't even be going to ICU.'

The poor fella had a permanent goose egg on the right side of his forehead from falling down all the time. He had built up such a pain tolerance form all he went through as a baby that nothing phased him. He thought he was Superman.

The surgery did improve his gait coordination about 25-30 %, so he didn't fall as often after that! But in general, elementary school was a struggle for Avery in many ways. It was difficult for him to sit still, and the stiffness in his right arm from cerebral palsy, made it impossible for him to print legibly. Thankfully we were able to get a laptop for him to do all his schoolwork.

As well, his imbalance and coordination from the cerebral palsy caused much frustration and any ability to perform physical activities with much success. Sports Day was a painful event. Avery would try so hard, but always fall. It broke my heart. He had the determination to be an athletic star, but his body couldn't follow it through. We would tell him that he didn't have to attend Sports Day, but he would have nothing to do with that, and wanted to give it his all!

One 1000 metre race he fell halfway through and began to cry. I didn't know what to do and was filled with despair for him. Then, suddenly one of the Dad's came running onto the field, puts Avery on his shoulders, and they race to cross the finish line. I still cry when I think about that story, and there were many spectators wiping their eyes that day too. (Thanks Remert)

However, with all of Avery's delays and setbacks, he never complained. He had to try twice as hard as the other kids to get half the results. I began to understand determination is not acquired; it's built in; we are born with it.

I am proud of Avery and all the other people in the world who have demonstrated such strength and will to overcome. Avery is now a healthy twenty-two-year-old, and we celebrate every day!

Bonnie was right!

I knew it was a miracle to be able to watch him grow through the years, and I never took one minute for granted. He lived for a reason and what a privilege he has become the most unique human being; so kind and generous, and always seeing the good in people.

Avery has a very old soul and has made up for all he put us through when he was younger.   I'm amazed at his maturity and respectfulness. In his younger years, I especially loved the looks from hairdressers, doctor visits, and dental assistants when he would ask if he could pick a treat for his sister too. Now when he goes to the store, he often brings home a little surprise for Jesse. He always asks how we are doing, and you can tell he has a sincerity in his eyes that he really cares. Every day I still get, 'I love you Mom, you're the best mom in the world.' And every day I still get hugs.

In 2016, Avery graduated with honors, and he won the Nelson Mandela Hardest Working student award. You can imagine me in the audience... tears flowing faster than the tissue could keep up.

Currently Avery is in his fourth year of university achieving his Bachelor of Arts degree, and working part time at Home Depot. He enjoys working there and they value his hard work. Quite a few times now he has won Employee of the Month. Whenever I go there to buy something, I always make mention that I'm Avery's mom because I love to hear their praising comments about Avery. Cam says I do it for my own ego boost, but I say, there is nothing wrong with wanting to hear positive comments about our children.

Jesse

For many years we had endless struggles raising Jesse. Her world was complete frustration and confusion. Having been diagnosed in the moderate to high spectrum of autism, nothing in her world made sense. It would be like plucking me out of Canada and taking me into a country where I didn't know the language.

The only thing that brought excitement and joy to her life was her best friend, Grandpa. Although she could speak only a few words at three, all she ever said was, 'go see Grandpa.' I had to take her there every day.

When Dad died, Jesse's world fell apart. She just didn't understand. At the time, Cam and I are separated from her while we are living in a trailer in the hospital parking lot, and now her best friend is gone too. At one-point Jesse said to my mom, "Grandpa, Mom, Dad, Avery all gone." The poor little thing thought we had all abandoned her. My pain for her was beyond words as I thought how on earth could we ever make this up to her. And my poor mom having to try and answer. We tried to explain Grandpa is in Heaven now, but for months she would go to Mom and Dad's house, walking through all the rooms calling out for him. I still cry thinking of her pain. I felt defeated so many times because I couldn't help her make sense of her world... I couldn't take away her pain and suffering.

Tantrums from frustration and not being able to communicate her wants and needs escalated even more once school started and initiated many trips to pick her up. When my phone would ring during the day, I didn't want to answer it, but knew I had to.

They say, God only gives you what you can handle, but I questioned that many times.

I reached out to so many doctors and specialists, read a lot of books, attended countless autism courses and conventions over the years, but they weren't much help. Finally, we were able to see a psychiatrist from Children's Hospital who specialized in autism when Jesse was Fourteen, and thankfully we received the help we needed! He prescribed Jesse some anxiety medicine, and this was when things started to turn around for the better.

For at least a few years prior to that I wanted to see if medication would help Jesse, but our pediatrician said she didn't need it! Dr. Sunny from Children's Hospital said she should have been on medication much earlier because she was riddled with incapacitating anxiety. Immediately we saw her panic ease, and with patience, along with more therapies, Jesse has become the happiest, most well-adjusted person.

I feel now that Jesse's autism doesn't limit her anymore, but instead enhances all she is. Her favorite things to do are giving to others.... especially serving Meals on Wheels to the seniors, working at the Salvation Army, and walking dogs at the SPCA. She also makes beautiful necklaces and bracelets to give out to all her friends. If you get a Jesse Gemmell piece of jewelry, you know you are a special person, and feel very lucky. She clearly has a lot of her great grandma in her! Especially because they both love taking care of seniors. If you are over eighty, Jesse will want to be your best friend. I always wondered why she loves babies and children so much, until I figured out; they never threaten her. Their gentleness and innocence provide a comfort for her.

She is also quite a ham bone and social butterfly, who brightens the days of all those around her. If you know here, you are lucky to see the most vibrant smile fill your heart with joy. It's fun to watch people's faces when she walks into a room. They can't help but grin from ear to ear. When the Handy Dart brings her home from her program, I love it when

I'm there to hear her giggling all the way from the bus to the house.

Occasionally I pick up Jesse from program, and I am always pleasantly surprised to see what Jesse is doing. Recently I picked her up and she was feeding her friend who is a quadriplegic. She was giving her one French fry at a time which took probably five minutes for each one.

One of my favorite stories was when she was in High School. One afternoon after she came home, I opened her lunch kit to clean it and I saw a copy of Bravery in it. I said, "Hey, Jesse, why is there a copy of Bravery in your lunch kit?" Her answer just melted my heart. "Well Mom, there is a boy I go to school with who can't read, so at lunch, I read Bravery to him." I still cry when I think about it. I also laugh because the pages about her are more worn than the others :)

Jesse just turned twenty-five, and still lives at home. In the future she may begin living part time at an assisted living home. But for now, I love having her here at home!

It was difficult for me when I came to understand Jesse will not marry or have children. Our expectations, our dreams for our children typically have an order. We hope our children first are healthy, then graduate, start a good career, become happily married, and have children. When my friend's daughters got married and then had babies, I felt very happy for them, and for brief moments I felt sad that I would not experience this joy with my own daughter. Thankfully, it never lasted long because I was fortunate enough to understand, what we cannot change, we must not grieve.

Jesse gave me the most wonderful gift when she inadvertently taught me it is our children's happiness we really want, not what our hopes for them are. I wouldn't change anything for the world.

We could all learn a few lessons from her generous personality and unconditional love.

Parents with special needs children have very different challenges, and had I not experienced it first hand, I couldn't have imagined all it encompasses. It can be exhausting, overwhelming, and insurmountable at times, but would I change one thing? Not even for a second do I hesitate; God blessed me with miracles.

Chapter Three
Me

"Share your smile with the world. It is a symbol of friendship and peace."

~ Christie Brinkley

An entire life course can be completely rerouted from a single circumstance... a single event. Although I wouldn't want to relive the trauma following Avery's birth, it has been the best experience in my life. Being a mother and raising a child is one of the most important jobs in the world. I've said many times, 'Anyone can have a child, but raising an honorable, respectful human being is what constitutes being a great parent.'

Avery and Jesse provided me with a unique and special opportunity for a greater ambition in life. Their portal of enlightenment gave me a new life's purpose to help people understand how life can be wonderful even though it doesn't go as we expected or planned.

People used to say things to me like, "Oh, you poor thing ... you have gone through so many struggles in your life." They didn't get it; they were feeling sorry for me, but I was feeling grateful and blessed. And that was okay because it further helped me understand why I had to write Bravery, and why I needed share my experience to renew faith in times of malaise.

What is interesting is how I almost didn't write my book because my pompous English Professor didn't think I had the writing talent. When we are young and impressionable, often insecure, we tend to believe what adults or professionals say.

Thankfully the notion to write Bravery never left me and I thought to heck with what anyone says, I've got to write this book. So, I did, and it was one of my most rewarding experiences. Not just because I pushed through my fears, but because I helped others open their eyes to enlightening new perspectives.

After I published Bravery, I donated partial proceeds to Children's Hospital. It was the right thing to do... giving back to the place and people who saved Avery's life.

Since I self-published, I had plenty of self-promoting to do, so I started to do some public speaking. In the beginning I was completely petrified to speak in front of audiences, and one day Avery said to me, "Mom, why do you want to do public speaking if it scares you so much?" It was a great question, and

Kim Gemmell

after thinking about it for a bit I said, "Well, I guess it's because my message is more powerful than my fear." It was a great revelation, and inspiration to keep going... even accomplishing a TED Talk.

Over the years I've had wonderful opportunities to work at some great places; Patient Consultant at two medical aesthetic clinics, Impact Speaker at United Way, and Fundraising Coordinator at the Heart & Stroke Foundation. All have allowed me the opportunity to feel blessed with the pleasure to support and help others! Cam says it's a good thing I don't change husbands like I do jobs. I can often be heard saying, "I'm still trying to figure out what I want to be when I grow up."

As you can imagine, I am a very overprotective mom, and had much anxiety for years. Shortly after Avery came home from the hospital, I was diagnosed with PTSD, which I kind of figured I had. I would rarely leave Avery, and when I would be out running errands and happen to hear or see an ambulance racing down the street, an instant panic would strike as I envisioned them coming for Avery. There were even a few times when I would try to follow the ambulance and put myself in danger.

However, in time I was able to wean myself off medication and find solace through exercise, meditation, and long walks every

33

day. Expressing my feelings through motivational speaking and blogs have been very therapeutic and good for my soul.

Approximately thirteen years ago I became an enamored student of The Law of Attraction, mostly through the teachings of Eckhart Tolle, Napoleon Hill, and Abraham Hicks. I focus on gratitude and being present in the moment as much as possible. Yesterday is gone, it's in our past, and tomorrow's out of sight. All we really have is right now; this moment. Of course, we must plan and such, but when we become more aware, we discover we fret about way too many things from our past or future that we can't control. This has helped me focus on the positives my life and weed out unnecessary negatives. It wasn't easy to get to this place, and that's why I felt the need to write this book. Most of the upcoming chapters are designed to provide more gratitude, fulfillment, peace within yourself, and the world around you.

I have managed to keep the promises I made in Bravery, especially this one; "If I ever get to bring Avery home, I will be the happiest mom in the world." Well, twenty-one years later, I still feel I am the most fortunate mom in the world.

My mom is doing very well, and continues to live in the house I was born and grew up in. She's in her late Seventies now, as ever, and fit as a fiddle. Golfing, curling and maintaining her big yard and gardens has kept her moving and healthy. It's hard to believe that this May will be 22 years since Dad's passing. I think about him every day and miss him so much. I still dream about Dad and Grandma, which provides a welcomed comfort. Mom never had another mate after Dad died, and she was only 56. I didn't think there would ever be a person that would measure up to him.

Cam and I are going on 29 years of marriage. We always did make a great team, but as we all know, a solid marriage takes hard work, and a little bit of luck finding a lovely person. Many years ago, I watched an interview with Joanne Woodward; Paul Newman's wife. The interviewer said, "How the heck have you been able to withstand a 50-year Hollywood marriage, especially to heart throb Paul Newman. Hollywood marriages don't have a history of longevity." Her answer surprised me but made perfect sense. Joanne said, "Well, I guess we're just lucky, we never fell out of love at the same time." Wow, I thought. Yes... there were times when I thought, who is this guy and what did I see in him? But I'm sure there were days when Cam thought the same. Our squabbles never lasted long, which I attribute to good communication. And fortunately, I married a great guy who loves me a lot and likes making me happy.

Cam's dad unfortunately died a slow death of lung cancer in 2010. The cancer going into remission for a short spell but returning in the brain a year later. Of course, were all devastated, especially Cam and his mom taking it very hard. It was a very devastating time for all of us, and I don't think my mother-in-law, Madge ever fully recovered from the loss. She lived for six years after that, but her health started slowly declining, and in 2018 suddenly dying of a brain bleed. It was so sad and terribly hard on Cam. He was very close to his mom, and as the wonderful son he was, checking in on her pretty much every day in her last year, and buying all her groceries.

Not too long ago I went to a medium a while ago when the lady began to talk about Dad and Grandma. She said my Grandma sends me four-leaf clovers and comes to me through all the birds who fly across my path. It was amazing to hear because I always have birds flying right pass me on my walks, and so close. I continue to find four-leaf clovers all the time, sometimes two or more in one day. I used to post photos on Facebook when I found them, but people started to think I was growing a four-leaf clover farm. I know they are messages from my grandma in Heaven, and it's a comfort to find them. Every time I do, I look up into the sky and holler thank you.

The medium asked if my dad always wore a baseball cap, and I said, "Yes always!" She also said he was with a newborn baby boy who passed away soon after birth. At the time I had no idea who that would be, but after talking to my mom about it, she said Dad had a brother that died right after birth! Mom only knew this from Dad's sister. He never spoke of it, or anything about his youth. When Mom and I went on a family reunion to Ireland, we found out that Dad's mom sent him and three of his seven siblings to an orphanage.

Smile Again

Chapter Four
When Bravery Arrived

"Because of your smile, you make life more beautiful."

~ Thich Nhat Hanh

I t was one of those days where you feel like pinching yourself to make sure you're not dreaming.

My girlfriend Tracee phoned me to chat and see how things were going and to say we should go see Oprah when she comes to town in a couple weeks. I said, "Yes, absolutely we should go." So that was that, the tickets were ordered.

It dawned on me, *Bravery* was expected to arrive a day or two after Oprah. 'Maybe the books will come early, and I can take a copy to Oprah. Maybe this is all a sign; Oprah and my book coming at the same time.' I chuckled, 'wishful' thinking.

It was early Wednesday evening, and the night before Oprah, however, no books yet.

Flopping on the couch for a moments reprieve before making supper and following our evening ritual, Mya my little four-pound fluffy hair Chihuahua who thinks she's a pit bull, alerts me that someone is approaching the door.

Wondering who would be coming at this time of the day, I open the door to a UPS guy resembling Doug from the TV show, King of Queens. With a pen in his mouth, he garbles, "Got ten boxes here for you. Where do you want them ma'am?"

What? Ten boxes! It must be my books!! What else could it be?

I thought my heart was going to burst out of my chest!! Five years of blood sweat and tears, and I am finally holding my book in my hand!! One of my friends said it must kind of feel like when you're pregnant; you know the baby is coming, but until you can see it and feel it, it doesn't seem real. I thought her analogy was pretty good. And it took me five years to have Bravery!

My new journey had officially begun, and I marveled at what wonderful possibilities it was going to bring. Me an author... who'd have thought?

Chapter Five
Our Crazy Oprah Adventure

"Nothing you wear is more important than your smile."
~ Connie Stevens

Thursday afternoon arrives, and I'm as prepared as I can be for what todays adventure may bring. Since Cam was out of town at a real estate convention, and I wouldn't be home until late, I decided to have the kids stay at their Grandma's house for the night. Madge took Jesse because she lives close to her school, and my mom took Avery because the bus comes right past her house.

I phoned Tracee to see if she was on schedule, and yes she was. Our plan was to get away early, just in case of any setbacks along the way. We figured 3.5 hours gave us more than enough time, with a little extra to grab a bite... or so we thought.

It was a nice clear sunny afternoon at 3:30 pm when Tracee arrives at my door. So off we go down the road with excitement in our chatter as we discuss what Oprah's venue may be like. About 10 minutes into the drive I blurt out, "Oh no Tracee, I forgot the bag of Jesse's pj's and clothes to drop off at Madge's.

"No worries." She said, "We have plenty of time, so let's just turn around and go back."

I couldn't believe it! I had even left the bag outside on my car hood so I would see it as I passed it in the driveway. Oh well, Tracee was right, we had lots of time. Oprah didn't start till 7:00 pm and it was a two-hour drive at the most.

Back on track and hitting the highway, we continue to chat about the anticipated evening ahead. About 45 minutes into our drive, it begins to rain. "Oh shoot!" Tracee says, "I forgot my umbrella."

"Oh no. I forgot mine too." I reply.

I had especially bought a little compact umbrella yesterday that I could put in my purse.

Needing to look our best for Oprah, and knowing we had a bit of a walk from the parking lot to the arena, we decide that once we are off the highway, we will stop at a store to pick one up. In theory that was a great plan, but once off the highway, we could only see a few stores that may carry an umbrella and they were on the other side of the road, and the traffic was too heavy to cross, and it would take a long time to get to the other side and back again.

Getting closer to our destination, there were a lot of sudden lane turns we needed to make, at least according to our GPS. Seeing us trying to find our way through this bustling city was quite comical. With Tracee's well maneuvered driving skills, we narrowly escaped a couple of fender benders. Other than a few cars honking at us, it was all good.

Time was getting tight, but we could see Rogers Arena in the distance, so we knew we were close. There would be no time to stop and get a bite somewhere and decide a hot dog at the arena would suffice. Crowds of people were filling the sidewalks, all making their way to see Oprah. One by one, we watch as their umbrellas began to pop up. Yes, the skies were opening, and the rain was beginning to fall hard.

"This is so not good." I yelled.

"I know!" She shrieks. "But there's nothing we can do about it now."
She was right, short of offering a lot of money to someone for their umbrella, which I seriously contemplated. But now, our

only focus was finding the Costco parking lot because it was the closest to the arena.

With Tracee paying all her attention on the road, and me looking at the GPS for guidance, we almost miss the Costco sign. It seemed to appear out of nowhere, but we are on the outside lane. She swiftly hit the brake pedal and turns on her blinker, but none of the drivers on the inside lane would let us in, and the drivers behind us were honking their horns, so we had no choice but to pass it!!

"What now?" Tracee shouted.

"I don't know!! Just keep going. We will have to go around the block and come back." I said.

Yes, once again, in theory this was a good idea, but when you have the blind leading the blind, not so much!! Somehow... someway, we got lost, and way off track. I can't believe it. What started off as a well-planned, properly executed day is falling apart.

At this rate, I wonder, am I ever going to get my book to Oprah???
Finally, we decided we had better stop and ask someone on the sidewalk for directions. At the next stoplight we see a

policeman on a bike. I roll down my window and say, "Excuse me sir."

He didn't hear me, so I told Tracee to pull up closer. Now I can tell he thinks we're trying to run him over and gives us a nasty look!! Great, that's all we need is to be hauled into the police station! We'd miss Oprah for sure.

Once I began to ask for directions, his frown disappears as he explains where we need to go. We weren't that far off course, so we thought we'd be okay. As we approach the arena, we realize that by now most of the parking lots would be filled up, so we decide to just park at the next lot we came across.

We knew we were close to the arena but not sure exactly how far. Once we make it to the sidewalk, we notice we are about three blocks down and two to the right. Yes, it's not that far if it weren't raining so hard that the water is bouncing four inches off the ground.

We begin to run in our high heel boots towards the stadium. I pull the scarf from my neck and wrap it around my head as we make our way. Tracee decides it's a great idea and does the same. We are laughing so hard we can hardly breathe!! I don't even care, I just want to get there.

I yell out to Tracee, "Why are we laughing? We should be crying. This is not how I want to look to see Oprah!!"

She can barely utter, "I know." Because she was laughing so hard too.

We make it to the entrance of the arena... I can hardly believe it! I snap a selfie of Tracey and I standing at the line up in front of the door. It was not a pretty sight; our faces dripping with water and mascara running down, and our hair soaked. (The scarves over our head didn't work as well as I hoped they would).

We had made okay time after all. A few minutes to try and dry off, fix up our makeup as best we can, and then off to our seats.

Our location was okay, close to the floor but near the other end of where Oprah would be. First thing Tracee says is, "How do we get your book to Oprah now??"

We scope the stadium thinking of a way.

"Go ask that security guard if he'll take it to the stage?" Tracee says.

"I don't think he will do that." I reply.

Tracee agrees. So now what???

I think to myself... I could get as close as possible to the stage and try to throw it up there. Then, thankfully realizing that's a dreadful idea.

I was sitting there, listening to the sounds of the huge crowd who are as excited as us to see Oprah, when something prompted me to get out of my seat and approach the security guy.

"Excuse me sir, do you think there is a remote possibility I could get this book to Oprah?"

He took the book, opened it up, looked up at me and said, "Is this a gift to Oprah?"

I sensed a bit of hope and was awkwardly nervous in my reply, "Yes, it is. See it's me on the cover." I don't know why I said that, but then he said, "Well, Oprah is accepting gifts, so I will pass it on."

What did he say??? Did he really say what I thought he said??

Why yes, I think he did. I passed him the book and turned back towards my seat wearing the biggest grin ever!!

Orpah's show was amazing!! Her wisdom, grace and humor filled the crowd with such positive energy. Her experience, and insights, inspired a newfound encouragement to be the best that we can be.

It was a very entertaining evening, and a very memorable one as well. Thanks Tracee.

I haven't heard from Oprah yet, but you never know!

Chapter Six
Launching Success

"Smile in the mirror. Do that every morning and you'll start to see a big difference in your life."

~ Yoko Ono

Over 200 people from the Lower Mainland came to attend my book launch and signing. Even people I didn't know, but who had heard through the paper and radio about the event. It was a very exciting day for me, and I must have changed my clothes about twenty times before deciding on a bright pink dress.

During the event I read a couple pages from the book, and you could hear a pin drop. When I looked up, I was surprised to see many people welling with tears, and thankfully I ended it on a positive note.

Avery was beaming with excitement as he sat beside me signing books too. Everyone was excited to talk to this little miracle of ours. I remember looking down the lineup of people and thinking, 'Wow, all these people are lined up to get a copy of my book.'

Some people stayed after the signing to talk to us. Quite a few wanted to share their story with me. It's one of the many wonderful aspects of telling our own story because it opens the path for others to share their own, and sharing is healing.

Publishing Bravery opened many exciting doors. I'll never forget my first radio interview. I have to say I was nervous to go on live radio and worried I may trip over my tongue. Walking into the tiny studio was very daunting... all kinds of technical equipment, wires, buttons and bells. But what I found most scary was putting on the huge headphones and the giant microphone staring me right in the face!

Sadie was the name of the morning host who interviewed me, and I was so amazed at how comfortable she made me feel. As soon as she said, "Okay, here we go," I felt calm, cool and collected. I couldn't believe that my answers flowed effortlessly from my mouth! It was easier than I thought.

Then there was the call I received from Global News television wanting me to come in for a live interview with Jill Kropp! I had only a few days to prepare and that freaked me out for a bit until I realized I really had nothing to be nervous. I know my story and my passion to tell it!

I was happy my mom wanted to come with me for the company. The interview was scheduled for 8:00 am, and we had to be there by 7:00 for hair and makeup and some interview prep time. Amid rush hour morning we'd have to leave our house by 5:00 am to ensure we wouldn't be late. That would mean getting up around 4:00 am. Coupled with probably not being able to sleep from the excitement, We decided to head into Vancouver the night before and stay at a hotel.

Arriving on time I was accompanied to the makeup room. I couldn't believe how much make up they put on me. I looked like a porcelain doll, but when I saw myself on camera, I looked okay. And fortunately, the interview went off without a hitch and I was thrilled.

Bravery had made a great start, and I was so pleased to be flooded with many wonderful emails and calls. Most saying how they loved reading Bravery and couldn't put it down.

I sent some of the main characters; Avery's primary nurse, Bonnie, Avery's head cardiologist, Dr. Human, and his heart surgeon, Dr. Leblanc, a copy of Bravery. I wanted them to know how it really feels from the other side. I needed them to know what we go through as parents of a sick baby, and how they are hero's in our eyes.

I was overwhelmed when I heard back from each of them. Collectively all saying how they were grateful for this story, and how they laughed and cried as they followed along our turbulent journey. It must have been an interesting perspective for them to see inside a parent going through a crisis and having to leave their baby in trust to them. Of course, all parents of sick children express sincere gratitude, but when you get an idea of what it's like to 'walk in one's shoes, ' through all the desperate hours, days, weeks and months, it's very powerful.

Chapter Seven
TEDx Talk

"Never forget to smile and appreciate yourself."

~ Debasish Mridha

When I saw an opportunity to apply to do a TEDx Talk in Chilliwack, I instantly knew I must try out. However, I found out the theme was Future Shapers, and I wondered how I could put a spin on my story to fit this theme. Most of the applicants had more scientific talks, and topics relating to our world advancing through technological breakthroughs. Yet, after some thought, it became very clear, I was a future shaper after all. My speaking events, blogs and posts are all about improving our quality of life and finding fulfillment and joy... that's future shaping alright!

I titled my talk, The Value of Human Connection – Unplugged. It was based on my beliefs of how our world is losing touch of valued relationships largely contributed by social media. For instance, although we may have over 500 or more 'friends' on Facebook, many of us are lonelier than ever. We are losing special relationships like our mentors. I use the example of all the wisdom and strength my Grandma gave me growing up, and how it saved me during my own crisis. Too many people are caught up in the virtual world, they neglect real people, real mentors.

There was a lot of other good speakers, and I wasn't sure if I would make it through. Waiting for the judges to announce after the try outs was agony, and they took a long time making their decisions. However, it was worth the wait when I heard my named called as crowd favorite. I had wanted this so much, and I think I jumped a foot off the ground. I remember Cam saying on the way home, "I was sure happy you made it through because I wasn't looking forward to the drive home if you didn't!"

I was surprised when weeks later I found an old manifestation wish list from three years earlier and doing a TED Talk was on it! I had forgotten all about that list.

The days leading up to my TED Talk were increasingly getting more anxious... What if I freeze? What if I forget part of my talk? There was so much to be nervous about, even though I was beyond prepared! I knew my talk inside and out, so why did my blood pressure skyrocket every time I thought about it?

I started to Google tips to ease panic and nerves before delivering a public speech... which is kind of ironic since some of my talk is about technology getting in the way of human connection. Except I do say... what we need is balance, and the internet can be a great resource.

I made a revealing discovery when I read that our fear can be based on a past incident that is not a conscious memory. This must have triggered something because I had a breakthrough discovery. I remembered standing in front of the class, when I was in grade one or two, and being asked a question. I don't remember the question, but I do remember being humiliated and feeling stupid when my teacher belittled me by making me feel dumb for not knowing the answer, and leaving me stand up front for what seemed like a painfully long and anguishing time. I remembered getting in trouble quite a bit and being sent to the time out cardboard train caboose, in the corner of the room. Then I recalled always pretending to be sick because of my fear to go to school. I wasn't a bad kid, but I had difficulty adjusting.

All over again, I could sense the feeling of humiliation and shame, and I knew that was why I was so petrified to stand in front of people and talk. It wasn't my incompetency or lack of intelligence at all... it was because of a mean old teacher. And that mean old teacher couldn't humiliate me anymore! It was a wonderful realization that allowed me to deliver my TEDx Talk with passion and conviction!

I'm grateful I pushed through all those years of fear to become a public speaker and reach as many people as possible. My message is more powerful than my fear! Now one of my passions is to speak at schools and tell all these bright eyed and ambitious young people to never let anyone squash their dreams! Never let anyone diminish their worth. If we feel a strong purpose and have the desire... then anything is possible, and any goal can be reached, no matter what anyone says.

Chapter Eight
It's Never Too
Late to Get Started

"Be the reason someone smiles. Be the reason someone feels loved and believes in the goodness in people."

~ Roy T. Bennett

Since I was able to break through the fear and procrastination trap to take that leap of faith, I'd like to share something's that helped me succeed.

Fear can stop us and heed us from doing something we want to do. Whether it's changing jobs because we are not happy, or a dream to sky dive, we often let the fear stand in our way, and our desires get shelved. This is a travesty because we are missing out on a much more enriched life just because of fear.

Fear is only a state of mind, and if we can shift our paradigm, we can see wonderful improvements. It's so easy for me to see now; however, that wasn't the case for most of my life. I was a big 'chicken!' Fear and procrastination held me back a lot, but it doesn't upset me to think about it now because we can't change our past. I'm just grateful it doesn't stop me now!

We've probably all been guilty of procrastinating at some point... why do today what we can put off until tomorrow? Then we get complacent, and nothing changes. Unless change happens, we will keep getting more of what we are putting out there. I used to be famous for saying "I just can't get caught up." Or, "There just isn't enough time in the day." Once I unearthed the repetitive pattern, I could change it, and it was as though a bunch of extra hours opened!

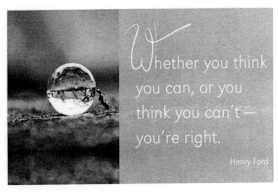

Whether you think you can, or you think you can't — you're right.

Henry Ford

I love this! Thank you, Henry Ford.

We are creatures of habit and we don't even realize it. We get so used to life being this way we somehow overlook that each day is a wonderful opportunity for change and/or growth. You will see many examples of this in later chapters. Look around at people you know, and you will see a pattern. The bad luck 'victims' keep getting bad luck; the prosperous continue with more prosperity. The negative people always find things to complain about; the positive people continue to have gratifying experiences, and rebound much quicker from the adversities that will come and go.

A great part of our life is consumed with school, work, and family. By the time we can lift our head and take a breath... we're in our fifties.

Largely our society is conditioned to believe that once we've hit middle age and beyond, it is too late for new endeavors! Whoever started this mindset couldn't be more wrong! It just may be more challenging to change because we've had to break through more years of conditioned behavior.

Many of the most accomplished people in the world didn't reach success until their later years. Thomas Edison had always dreamed of creating a lamp that gave off light. Well, it took him over 10,000 failed attempts before he discovered electricity, and he was well past the middle of his life. Can you even imagine? 10,000 attempts! Wow, now that is some perseverance!

One of the most famous presidents of all time, Abraham Lincoln, who was arguably one of the best presidents the United States has ever seen, was a failure at the hands of many careers before he became president. He failed at farming. When he turned to politics, he lost the nomination to run for U.S. senate. Twice, he was defeated in the run for U.S. Congress. And he was defeated in the run for the nomination of Vice-President. Indeed, there were even more failures before he became President of the United States.

So, for all of you who feel time has passed you by – think again! I have a 76-year-old friend who has started her book, and another 84-year-old friend who still plays on a baseball team!

It just goes to show, if we want something bad enough, we must NEVER say never. Never give up and most definitely do not listen to the discouraging naysayers!!

Here are 8 simple ideas for getting started and staying motivated, some of which will be greater explained in upcoming chapters.

1 ~ Surround yourself with as many positive people as you can. Like attracts like. Do you ever notice how your positive mood changes if you're in the vicinity of a negative or grumpy person? Sometimes it's unavoidable in certain situations like our workplace or family members we don't get along with, but in environments where you do have a choice – let's choose to be around positive uplifting people because it's contagious. (I talk about toxic people in chapter 14.)

2 ~ Filter out negativity and discouragement that comes our way. I always remind myself that how we react to negativity or discouraging people is in our control. One of the phrases I try to remember to say every morning is, "It's my decision, and I'm not going to allow anyone to interfere or negatively affect this beautiful day for me!" This usually takes some time and patience, especially for people like me who have always been quite sensitive, often taking things too personally. If this is the case, keep persevering. It's well worth it and very gratifying when we can let negativity and criticisms bounce off us like we are wearing a bullet proof vest.

3 ~ Exercise more. Regular exercise including cardiovascular activity and strength endurance is a terrific boost for feeling good about ourselves and stimulates those feel-good endorphins! Our immune system is strengthened and overall, we are much healthier physically and mentally.

No excuses like, "I don't have time." This excuse drives me nuts! We can always find a half hour or an hour of time to do one of the best things we can possibly do for our body. Our quality of life depends on it. So, skip the Seinfeld rerun that you have already seen 3 times and get moving. It's that easy, and you'll feel so much better!

4 ~ Get your blood levels checked. Doctors are finding out more and more how middle-aged men, and especially woman are lacking in protein. As well, slower thyroid issues can arise, which be very energy depleting. Good energy is key to staying motivated.

5 ~ Be kinder to yourself. Don't ruin your day if you fall off your diet, missed an important appointment or a workout. We are humans who will make mistakes and errors sometimes. Getting upset with ourselves only prolongs the bad feelings and takes longer to get on track. I'm happy to have discovered this ideology because I used to dwell on my mistakes for days, and it was completely counterproductive. LET IT GO!

6 ~ Read more non-fiction motivational books rather than fiction, or time-wasting tabloids. Search online to find topics that interest you or find things to learn of which you feel you could benefit from. Fisher Centre for Alzheimer's states reading is great exercise for the brain and can stave off dementia.

7 ~ Try to get outdoors more. Being in nature arouses our senses, and literally 'smelling the roses' will help us feel better too! The next time you are on a walk and enjoying beautiful scenery, pay attention to your mood. You'll probably notice it is in a more satisfying, peaceful place.

8 ~ It's important to make daily affirmations about our attributes and all we are grateful for. Being a long-time student of The Law of Attraction, I know how thoughts become things. This is even more forthright when we attach the feeling of excitement for all we must be grateful for (I have a whole chapter about this).

We will never be exempt from bad days; adversity will touch us all. There have been days for me where I just simply didn't feel grateful for anything, yet I have lots to be grateful for. But when I tried to focus, I could always find something, even if it's something so simple as having my eyes to see the beautiful bird flying by, or the legs that carry me to my destination. We can always find something to be grateful for.

Smile Again

64

Chapter Nine
Interpretations

"When Irish eyes are smiling, all is right with the world."

~ Irish Proverb

We all see life through different lenses, which is a good thing, otherwise we'd all be the same. How boring would that be. But interpretations can be so varied and completely opposite from one person to another. Is the cup half full of half empty?

I like to use success for an example. What does success mean? It's impossible to answer because it means different things to everyone. Just as beauty is in the eye of the beholder, so is success! We shouldn't pay any attention to what others define as success, because it's what we think of ourselves that really matters. What anyone else thinks of us need not contain any merit. Of course, we take into consideration what some people think, especially one's we have a relationship with, but no one's opinion determines our worth. Only we have that right.

What success is to one person, may be considered as a failure by another. Many people say it took Thomas Edison 10,000 failed attempts before he invented Electricity. He said he didn't fail; it just took 10,000 tries'! By the way, his teachers said, 'he was too stupid to learn anything.'

There are people I know who don't believe they are successful because they don't have their dream house, or a million dollars in the bank. Well, if that's what they believe, then they are not successful. Then there are those who live very modestly but feel great success and fulfillment.

I know two people with the same health challenges. One is always positive and makes the best out of every day, finding the silver lining, while the other feels cheated, and always in doldrums. It's interesting how both are similar age, have similar backgrounds with great support networks, but both have the complete opposite disposition and perception.

For a time, I felt unsuccessful. I had not fulfilled my original life desires. My role as a parent was not the one I originally planned or hoped for. No one wishes to have a baby born with a critical illness. No one plans on having a child with autism. We are not naturally educated or equipped to deal with something out of the norm, or unexpected. I could have felt sorrowful and probably no one would have blamed me.

But thankfully, I realized I was more fortunate than I could have ever hoped for. I'm blessed and uniquely special for the opportunity to raise my amazing children, who have made me a better person.

Even though interpretations are our very own to decide and determine, we often develop certain ones from the influences in our environment, whether it be our parents, teachers, TV, magazines, or whatever. Don't let someone else's ideology become yours. We have the control of our own interpretations, so be easy on yourself and others. The cup is always half full!

We determine our own perception whether we are rich or poor, young or old, sick or healthy. Once we truly understand this, we can live the best years of our life. Some of the richest people are miserable, and some of the poorest are happy.

After all, whatever frequency we are vibrating in, we will get more of... so let's choose the positive ones and see what happens!

Our life isn't a condition, it is a choice, and it is never too late to change your route!

Smile Again

Chapter Ten
Wally

"Each and every second of your day is the most valuable precious one you will get, so spend those seconds with a smile upon your face, and laugh."

~ Amber Hope

I'm so happy to have the 'Wally' story to share with you. A couple years ago, I was on my regular bike ride through the suburbs of Little Mountain and the path along the graveyard. I love this route because there are many beautiful mountains and trees all around, with various kinds of birds chirping in their own distinct language, and the hills are great exercise. I always find great adventures on my travels, whether it be meeting new people, seeing some deer munching on leaves, or often finding positive affirmations from the Universe like feathers and four-leaf clovers. Each time brings something new, and I always look forward to what may unfold; it is one of my favorite things to do!

Well, this day was exceptionally memorable. Making my way through the path at the graveyard I happened to see an old and dear friend of the family, who was one of my dad's best friends, named Wally. He reminded me of Dad, and how the anniversary of his death had just passed... 19 years.

Wally was sitting on the passenger side of a vehicle parked on the side of the road. I hadn't seen him for years, but we recognized each other right away. I jumped off my bike and went over to give him a big hug. I asked him what he was doing here, and he said his grandson was placing some flowers on his wife's grave for him. Since his own health was failing, he couldn't make it up the hill to her resting place.

It was so great to see him. We reminisced about many wonderful memories and for a moment it felt like my dad was alive again. Wally has always been a very jovial, fun-loving adventurous person, and it was so good to see him that day. As we laughed about some great stories his eyes took on a somber gaze. He paused for a moment then said, "Your dad and I lived a hell of a life. Now I'm an old man and can't breathe without this damn oxygen tank. I don't have any regrets though, but I want to tell you one thing, please don't stay mad at anyone... it's not worth it. Life is too short, and our time goes by so fast." Then he wiped a tear from his eye with his sleeve.

I don't know what prompted his thoughts, but they were the words I needed to here at this time, and they sunk to my core like a lead weight. On this hot summer day, Wally's 90 years of wisdom gave me goosebumps, and I will do my best to live by his advice. Finding gratitude has come naturally to me, but I need to value and celebrate that feeling more.

As his grandson returned, I said hello, then thanked Wally for our wonderful visit, and we said our goodbyes. Just before I started to ride off Wally said, "Hey Kim, say hi to your mom for me; I haven't seen her for years. Maybe you guys could come for a visit sometime."

I said, "You bet, she'd love that!"

I cried most of the way home thinking about my chance meeting with Wally, and his words echoed... Don't stay mad at anyone. Such simple words, but powerful ones that made me see just how right he was. That meeting of chance wasn't a coincidence, and our conversation changed me.

However, wherever... someone ... or something reaches your soul and changes us.

Wally passed shortly after I saw him, but my mom and I did get the chance to visit him before he died, and we had a game of crib. Most every day that summer I rode up to the gravesite to water his wife's flowers. On the days we went camping I asked my graveyard worker friends if they could water for me. We kept that plant alive all that hot summer.

I don't believe there is such thing as coincidence, and when we are ready... when we are open to receive the wonderful gifts from the Universe, we will be amazed at where our adventures take us and where gratitude will find us. Be alert and pay attention for your own 'Wally' encounter.

Chapter Eleven
Law of Attraction

"A woman is most beautiful when she smiles."

~ Beyoncé

The Law of Attraction (LOA) is the belief that the universe creates and provides for you that which your thoughts are focused on. It is believed by many to be a universal law by which "Like always attracts like." The results of positive thoughts are always positive consequences. It sounds simple in theory but it's not. Only a slim portion of our population can use it effectively. There are so many factors which need to be in place for any chance of success. It's not like... poof... we get it by simply asking.

That which we give our attention to, we will get more of... whether it is good or bad. This is not 'rocket science', we see it every day. Think about your own circumstance, or people you know, and you'll see some great examples of this.

To tell you the truth, I didn't know what to think of it all when I heard about this Law of Attraction philosophy in the early 2000's. It didn't resonate with me, and it took some time before I wanted to know more. Then for some reason, and I don't know why, but my interest to find out more perked. I started reading books and online recordings which soon led me to become a big follower. I had no idea that since 1877, The Law of Attraction had existed, but not until the late nineties did it begin to increase in popularity. It's been coined different names over the years, most popular being the publication of, 'The Strangest Secret' by Earl Nightingale in 1957.

Feeling grateful, optimistic, appreciative, and focusing on the present are the most common denominators to manifesting more goodness in our life. If we can obtain that state of gratefulness in our life, more things to be grateful for will come. But how can we feel gratitude if our life is in peril? That question had me stuck for quite some time until I realized I was inadvertently practicing gratitude during the ultimate worst time of my life when my dad died while Avery was very sick and fighting for his own life. Then my beautiful little girl is diagnosed with autism. One would think, 'How on earth do you find gratitude here???'

This was what was going on in my mind:

'Avery is still alive...he's fighting hard. He has the best surgeon in Canada ~ I'm finding four-leaf clovers everywhere and I

know they are messages from Grandma in Heaven saying everything is going to be alright. ~ Jesse may have autism, but she is healthy and beautiful from the inside out. ~ Although my dad was only 59, I was blessed with 32 beautiful amazing years with this most unique and strong human being. He gave me the character and hutzpah to make the best of life. He walked me down the aisle at my wedding and I have the best photo of us ever. The look in his eyes as he is dancing with me shows the love and admiration that fill my heart with joy every time, I look at it.

We really have more power than we know, and anyone, no matter what they are going through, can tap into theirs.

» If we always do what we've always done, we'll always get what we already have. So, keep an open mind to new desires.

» Be kind, be generous. Our actions naturally have a boomerang effect. History and Quantum Physics prove this. Good things never generally come from being selfish. One way or another karma will find its way.

» Feel as though we have already received our desire. A tricky part of The Law of Attraction for me to follow was believing what I have asked for is already here... why would I ask for it if I already had it? I was confused until I understood we just have put our self in the in emotional state of how it would feel to already have it. (We get more of what we pay attention to.) I visualize it like I'm making my own wine, all the steps have been carried out, and now it's just a matter of time before it's ready to drink. I can sense aroma and taste already.

I remember Oprah and Jim Carrey in an interview about his belief in The Law of Attraction. Jim said he visualized being a sought-after popular actor, and in the early nineties wrote a cheque to himself for ten million dollars and dated it around Thanksgiving 1995. Just before Thanksgiving that year, he signed a contract for ten million for his role in Dumb and Dumber.

One of the first exciting examples of The Law of Attraction conscientiously working for me was when Avery and I were going to the Bon Jovi concert in Vancouver. This was thanks to my sister-in-Law, Lorrie, for giving me two tickets as Christmas presents. I was super excited because I'm a huge fan of John Bon Jovi, and Avery was also excited because it was his first concert and he was 14 years old.

As we were driving down the highway on our way to pick up Cam's brother Paul and his wife Tanya, who had also bought tickets, Avery and I were having a great time anticipating the fun evening we were about to have.

I turned to Avery and said, "Remember how I have been talking about the book, The Secret, and what we put out into the Universe, we get more of the same back? How positive people are generally happier and more successful than negative people?"

Avery said, "Yes, I remember." So, I said, "Okay, well let's get really, really excited about today because something really amazing and special is going to happen to us... Let's believe it with all our might, feel it happening, and know for sure it will be true!"

By this time Avery is grinning from ear to ear and I couldn't tell if he was totally on board, or just thought I was a crazy mom!

We picked up Paul and Tanya and went for a bite to eat before the concert. They were teasing us how we had seats in the 'nosebleed' section at the very back of the arena, and how they had much better, closer seats on the second level.

It didn't really matter much to me, and I wasn't going to let anyone 'buzz kill' my excitement. Avery whispered to me, "Mom, what do they mean, nosebleed section?"

I giggled and wondered how to respond. After a few seconds I replied, "well that's what some people call the seats that are way up high, and sometimes people get nosebleeds at high altitudes, they're just teasing; we're not that high up."

On the way to our seats, Paul and Tanya said they would ride up the elevator with us to find our seats and then go back down to their own. As we were walking, Avery quietly says to me, "Mom, I see why they call this the nosebleed section."

Then... something interesting happened. A guy riding in the elevator with us said, "I hear you don't have the greatest seats... Do you want these floor tickets next to the stage?" Avery and I gave each other a perplexed look and we didn't know just what to say.

Then he said, "I'm in promotions with the band and have a few extra floor tickets." And he handed them over.

What??? Wow!! We thanked him very much, and I'm sure our expressions of excitement were thanks enough! Paul and Tanya had a funny stunned look on their faces as I said, "Okay, I guess we are going back down." ... Got to love karma.

What was most priceless for me that evening was the look on Avery's face as we walked down to the floor, about 4 rows from the stage, and he said, "WOW Mom... The Law of Attraction really does work!!"

We had a fabulous evening and a great story to tell for years.

If the Law of Attraction is new to you, and you'd like to begin practicing it, start with little things in order to make things believable to you. I started with saying how lucky I was to always find a sale on what I wanted to buy. And, I always pick your fastest line ups. Feel like you have placed the order and it's on its way. Don't get discouraged if it takes a bit of time, just keep practicing!

The next few chapters are helpful to achieve success with manifesting, but also, provide anyone with support, and tidbits of advice to change perspectives. If you keep an open mind, you'll experience some great things behind new doors.

Smile Again

Chapter Twelve
EGO

"When you detect egoic behavior in yourself, smile. At times you may even laugh."

~ Eckhart Tolle

go is an interesting word, even the sound of it is obscure. I used to think the definition was simple; people who thought they were better than anyone else. Someone who had a 'big head.' It wasn't until I read Eckhart Tolle's, The Power of Now, that I really understood what the ego was all about, and realized it is much more diverse than I thought. In fact, it was a complete game changer. The way I look at people and things are very different, and my own behavior has greatly changed in a much better way. Even though I've always tried to not judge or compare because it's nonproductive and self-depredating, I saw I had some improving to do!

Eckhart Tolle's dissection of ego is delivered in a brilliant, relatable interpretation:

"The most common ego identifications have to do with possessions, the work you do, social status and recognition, knowledge and education, physical appearance, special abilities, relationships, personal and family history, belief systems, and other collective identifications. None of these is you."

Just as a fish lives his entire life in the water, most of humanity lives their entire life in the ego personality. The fish doesn't know anything about the water, unless a fisherman captures him and pulls him onto dry land. The fish flops and wiggles and seeks desperately to return to the water. A human being doesn't know that he or she is immersed in an ocean of ego (their own and everyone else's) unless some rare and unusual experience pulls them out of it into a higher or deeper dimension of experience. Usually, this experience is welcomed, but after a little while, we start to squirm and flail about in discomfort. We long to return to the safe confines of the ego mind.

We secretly love our ego because it gives us our identity. Without the ego and its rich and varied content, we feel as though we are nothing at all. We may even feel that we don't exist. The ego provides us our sense of identity through objects we own that make a statement about who we are: a nice car, a beautiful home, pretty clothes, the newest electronic gadgets etc,. We surround ourselves with objects that make us feel good about ourselves and make us look good to others. Many of the things that we buy and own are simply 'identity enhancers.' How many purchases have you made based on the reason that the item will improve your status or popularity?

The ego also provides us our sense of identity through its attachments to qualities we may have. "I am intelligent, I am a star athlete, I am a talented painter, I speak four languages, I am the tallest boy in my school, I am the prettiest girl in my family, I am an engineer for a top-secret space project, I am an award-winning journalist."

Ego is our identification with form, ideas, status, talents and even events. Many of us live, trapped, in the surface level of these identifications. This is a cause of great suffering because so much we identify with can and will change. The beautiful girl will eventually grow older and lose her looks. The athlete will eventually surpass his prime and lose his edge.

It's very important that we recognize what we are attached to, and that it will change. We must bring a deeper dimension of meaning into our lives so that we're not doomed to suffer the trappings of the shallow surface level of living, which will someday let you down.

So how do we free ourselves from ego?

One way to approach this is to work away on the attachments and identifications. We let go of this attachment and that attachment. We discover everything we're identified with and work to dis-identify with those things. This is a slow process, and by itself it will take a long time to attain. But it is a vital part of the awakening process, and if you seek every day to be less attached and less identified, it will immediately begin to improve the quality of your life and consciousness.

When I began to understand it this way, I realized I needed to change my outlook, and ever since then, I fully understood what peace felt like. I'm not always living in a state of peace yet, but I'm getting there.

A good analogy for me was my house. We've been living at our house for about sixteen years, and I had wanted to move for about 10 of those. Our house isn't ugly, I just wanted a newer, bigger one, plus, we used to move every few years because I found it exciting to buy a new home to live in. Well, Cam did not want to move anymore. It was tense with us, and at times at times I was bitter. 'Why does he get to have his way? Because he's the bread winner of the family?'

Cam wanted to do some home improvements instead of moving, but I said no. Why would we make all these nice changes in our house if I was going to get my way at some point and move. I believe I felt this way because it was the only way I could show any little control I felt I had.

Cam didn't want to have a bigger mortgage, which was a valid reason to stay, but at the time I was only thinking what I wanted. So, I would make little digs all the time that would cause heated arguments. We were often unhappy, and I knew we were heading for separation if something didn't give.

Then, the timing of what the Universe delivered was marvelous. I learned about ego and its damaging effects. I discovered the destructive ego in me. Attachments and control! Ughh! That was a humbling revelation, but so fantastic at the same time.

Change did not happen overnight, old habits are hard to die, but in time I began to lose the attachment to bigger, better, nicer, etc.

Slowly we started doing some minor improvements to our house, which was a good compromise. Cam and I rarely have arguments now, but If we do, they don't last. Sure, I'd still consider moving, I've always loved an ocean view, but for now,

I'm very happy, and more importantly, at peace. This is the perfect state we want to be in to allow more good stuff to come.

When we don't know we need fixing, we'll never get fixed. This is one of the reasons I was inspired to write **Smile Again**. So many people walk around in a state of unhappiness, and they just don't know how to change it, or that it's even possible! Their ego is not in check, they are not aligned, and probably not in a place where they are feeling a lot of gratitude.

I am astonished at how this awareness made such a beautiful adjustment to my mindset and attitude about myself as well as others.

Chapter Thirteen
The Power of Presence

"If you smile when no one else is around, you really mean it."
~ Andy Rooney

There is another way to help free ourselves from the ego: presence. The present moment is the easiest exit point out of the ego. The ego can't co-exist with presence. The ego only lives in past and future. When you are present in this moment, there is no past or future, there is only now.

Once we understand ego, and adjust accordingly, we can begin to look at other ways to finding more fulfillment by living in the present more often. Letting go of old stuff that we can't change is freeing because we detach unswerving negativity from past events.

Eckhart Tolle was the person who guided me to this realization and new way of thinking when I read his book, The Power of Now. Prior to this writing he had been dealing with severe depression, and I think was the beginning of his motivation to write such a brilliant book. He spent a lot of time getting to the root of his depression and was able to conclude the answer was himself. Or, rather, the "self" his mind had created. Once he took that vision of himself away, he knew that it didn't really matter who he was. It simply mattered that he was, and that his past and future didn't define who he is in the present. In fact, shedding himself of the past and future was what finally led him to happiness.

He believes living in the present moment is the key to ending suffering for the following reasons:

The Past can fill us with regret. There is no way to change the past, but we often find ourselves fruitlessly fretting about it. How can this serve us well? It can't, and in fact can make us more miserable.

The Future can fill us with anxiety, especially in the Covid-19 pandemic we are enduring. The future is unknown, no matter what anyone says. Of course, it's a good idea to plan and be prepared for certain things, but dwelling and guessing about the unknown, is pointless and depleting.

Tolle acknowledges a balance is key. The past and the future should act as tools to help us make decisions, rather than be the driving force behind them. Our past gives us wisdom to draw on. Our future provides inspiration. It's kind of simple when we see how the present is the only time we have any control.

When I started to practice living in the now, it was an interesting experience and a very challenging one in the beginning. To change all my 53 years of conditioning was difficult, because I was brought up with a lot of emphasis on the past and the future. I wasn't conscious that living in the present was of value. I would however persist to learn, somehow knowing it would be worth the effort... to be completely satisfied with what I have, and not want more, more, more, would be so freeing and welcoming.

The easiest way for me to start being more present was on my nature walks. Listening to the birds, watching squirrels scurry around and climb trees, feeling the sun on my face (or rain), and smelling the fresh air. Even the sound of my footsteps as the earth rustled beneath my feet became a joy.

What started out as just a few moments began to increase. Slowly, I was able to gravitate to that spot of being present a little more often. It felt like a little celebration when I began catching my thoughts focusing uselessly on the past or future, and quickly change my frequency.

» Awareness is key to breaking old patterns. Old patterns run deep and are hard to change direction. It's normal for our mind to wander back to its way of thinking, but being aware and catching it when it does, is a great start.

» Worry can be a deal breaker when it is a constant feeling in our life. Being legitimately concerned about something is not the same as constant worry about things we cannot control. Reserve your concerns to things you can make a difference about and let go what is unswerving. My mom would always worry when I would go out at night when I lived at home. From the moment I left to the moment I returned she worried. I couldn't understand why she would ruin her evening about something that was not in her control. When Avery got his license, I temporarily slipped into her mode of thinking. Only, I justified it with thinking, 'well, this is different. With all that we went through with Avery, I'm allowed to feel this way.' Thankfully I persisted because I somehow knew it would be worth the effort. It is very freeing to be satisfied with what we have, and not want more, more, more.

» Slow down. We put too many expectations on ourselves which are unrealistic and promote stress. We will never find any degree of joy and peace if we are feeling angst or stress. Especially overachievers can easily get into the habit of focusing on what we need to do next, and never take a break to enjoy the present.

» Don't multitask. That can become overwhelming and focusing on one task at a time makes it easier to stay present. Be kind to yourself. Instead of getting mad at yourself for not getting all on your to do list tackled on time, say to yourself, 'Actually I accomplished quite a bit today.' Or, 'Well there is always tomorrow.'

» Meditation is presence at its best by acting as a tool for grounding us by focusing on our breathing as our lungs expand and contract oxygen. There are many benefits other than helping us stay present when we meditate for even as little as five minutes per day. The biggest advantage seems to be the reduction of stress and negativity. Research also shows how meditation can fight premature aging, give us more energy, pump up our immune system and much more.

Don't get discouraged if you find your mind wandering on different matters, that is common and happened to me often in the beginning. Once you realize you have wandered off, just let that thought go and return to the focus on your breath.

The best way to get started is sourcing out some of the guided meditations online that look appealing to you.

Learning the value of living in the now and practicing living in the present more often has been like a new lease on life for me. Many aspects have greatly improved, especially a more peaceful state of mind has emerged.

I hope to meet Eckhart one day to thank him! I was excited to learn he lives in Vancouver.

Chapter Fourteen
Clear the Way

"A smile is the light in your window that tells others that there is a caring, sharing person inside."

~ Denis Waitley

There was a lot of preparation before I could see any success to be more present. It's not as easy as turning our thoughts on or off.

As I previously mentioned, we have been conditioned to behave and become set in our ways over the years. Our parents, friends and many other people have been the main source of influence in our lives. Very often we follow the same pattern as those who raised us, or the ones we are around most often. So, if we have a desire to make changes for the better in our life, if we wish to shift our paradigm, it certainly can be done but not typically overnight.

The biggest obstacle for me, and others I know, was letting people get in our way.

There are some people in our life that we don't particularly see eye to eye with. Family members, coworkers, acquaintances, and even people we don't know like politicians. Geezzzz, every time my mom says the name of a certain government official, her blood pressure rises. I used to be the same because I emulated my family's behaviors. However, now I can finally say and practice successfully, 'I don't let anything, or anyone negatively affect me, especially if I have no control to change it.' If we can apply this thought process, we will find more ease and contentment in our life.

As well, if people express angst against us, it often has very little to do with us. It's their own frustrations being taken out on others. I don't get along very well with complainers, or negative people because I'm not in that category of cynical people. But I don't have to let them bother me with their behavior. Another person's attitude or composition has nothing to do with me. I cannot change it and therefore I mustn't give it my energy. When I started applying this philosophy, I didn't take things so personally, or let affect me negatively. Instead I thought, 'Wow, I am sure happy I am not walking around with a chip on my shoulder.'

Some people are extremely closed-minded and impossible to talk to, but we still need to communicate with them. When I find myself in a situation with someone who just can't hear me in the moment, I don't force the issue. Trying to get my point across to someone that can't hear me only escalates the situation. Sometimes the clearest form of communication is silence.

My good friend Ken Popove is the Mayor of our city and I have to say how proud of him I am. We all know we can't please everyone all the time, but we do our best to do what is right. Dealing with the homeless challenges, mental health concerns, among many others, and now the Covid-19 pandemic, our politicians and mayors have a challenging job. I admire the way Ken deals with everything with such a levelheaded sense of resolve. He manages to not let any negative opinions or propaganda hinder or affect him or his duties. As with all mayors, a lot of fingers point blame their way, and Ken gets his share. I'm sure it's challenging at times, but he lets it go, and doesn't let it get in his way to continue serving our city with ardent devotion.

Whether we have a lot of malice to deal with, or a little, we all have the power not to let someone else's behaviors or actions bring us down. Contrary to what many believe, we can find happiness and contentment when we have some unavoidable negativity around us.

Wayne Dyer said it best:

HOW PEOPLE
TREAT YOU
IS THEIR KARMA
HOW YOU REACT
IS YOURS

~ Wayne Dyer

The Inspiration Network

We know we can learn ways to live with the people we'd rather not, but if there are people we are around that don't need to be, let them go. If it's a hostile, abusive spouse, leave. If it's a depredating, cruel boss, look for a new job. Those are just a couple of examples, but if you are suffering at the hand of another, get out! In some situations that can be very challenging to do but necessary to improve our life and others even theirs because we stop being their enablers.

There are some people that we just can't help, no matter how hard we try, and it will drive us crazy to continue living Groundhog Day.

An imperative task to find any improvements and obtain more abundance in our life is clearing out the cobwebs. By this I mean overcoming old emotional wounds, which Eckhart Tolle coins 'the pain body'. This was a fascinating discovery for me, and important to understand before being free and living in the present could occur more often.

Eckhart says the pain body lurks in the corners of our mind. It is a mass of all our fears, insecurities, and negative thoughts that we lock away. It's the negative voices that have told us bad things about ourselves, which we ended up internalizing and mimicking when cornered.

"The pain-body wants to survive, just like every other entity in existence, and it can only survive if it gets you to unconsciously identify with it. It can then rise, take you over, "become you," and live through you. [The pain body] ... needs to get its "food" through you. It will feed on any experience that resonates with its own kind of energy, anything that creates further pain in whatever form: anger, destructiveness, hatred, grief, emotional drama, violence, and even illness. So, the pain-body, when it has taken you over, will create a situation in your life that reflects its own energy frequency for it to feed on. Pain can only feed on pain. Pain cannot feed on joy. It finds it quite indigestible".

This is so true, but all these years I never looked at it this way, I just never thought to look deep enough to see how and why I am the way I am and feel the way I do. It is an exhilarating experience to identify with this thought process and begin to release the pain body!

"The pain body, which is the dark shadow of the ego, is actually afraid of the light of your consciousness. Its survival depends on your unconscious identification with it, as well as on your unconscious fear of facing the pain that lives in you. But if you don't face it, if you don't bring the light of your consciousness into the pain, you will be forced to relive it again and again. The pain body may seem to you like a dangerous monster that you cannot bear to look at, but I assure you that it is an insubstantial phantom that cannot prevail against the power of your presence. So, the pain body doesn't want you to observe it directly and see it for what it is.

The moment you observe it, feel its energy field within you and take your attention into it, the identification breaks. A higher dimension of consciousness has come in. I call it presence. You are now the witness or the watcher of the pain-body. This means that it cannot use you anymore by pretending to be you, and it can no longer replenish itself through you. You have found your own innermost strength. You have accessed the power of Now".

What helped me wrap my head around all this was to equate the pain body to a bully. A negative entity that wants to demean and diminish. This was a fantastic progression for me and made living in the present come much more naturally, and ever so fulfilling!

If the pain body lives in you - dormant or active, becoming aware of it and understanding it has no purpose, then you can release it.

Once we clear the way of our own past and other distortions in our life, the clouds lift, and we can see where we are going and be much more efficient and productive along the way.

Smile Again

Chapter Fifteen
Alignment

"Just one smile immensely increases the beauty of the universe."

~ Sri Chimnoy

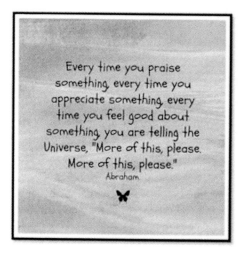

Every time you praise something, every time you appreciate something, every time you feel good about something, you are telling the Universe, "More of this, please. More of this, please."

Abraham

I love this quote from Abraham Hicks, and it sums up what alignment means in a simple sentence. It is a little more involved to put into practice, but when you do, it's a domino effect of more bliss.

Once we've squashed ego, dissolved the pain body, and have begun to understand how to live in the present, we are becoming aligned with the Universe, and at peace with our self.

Our state of alignment can change from moment to moment, and from subject to subject. We can feel nervous about money but confident in our physical health, for example, or we might feel empowered after we achieve a goal but disempowered when yet another problem surfaces.

We can also think of alignment in terms of inspiration. It isn't just feeling good, we enter a state in which the actions flow naturally, and we always seem to know the next best step to take.

Science calls this a state of flow and is the feeling of being "in the zone." Abraham refers to this state as inspired action.

When I came across an article about Abraham's advice to align with *source energy, I knew I had to share it because it is an easy, simplified, and very doable way to reap the joys of aligning.

*Source Energy ~ The conscious energy that creates what we want in the non-physical and we allow that in the physical through our alignment with source. Source energy is conscious enough to focus, create, and attract. We are fortunate enough to be able to consciously apply our will to direct source energy and attract what we want.

How to Align with Source Energy in Five Steps:

Step 1: We Experience Contrast

The first step in the process is the act of experiencing contrast. Contrast, according to Abraham, is any negative experience you encounter.

As we live our normal life, we will always find things we do not prefer, or have ideas about how our life could be better. Whether we express this desire as a complaint or a wish, it represents our natural expansion and desire for growth.

This step happens automatically, every day of our life, even when we are not aware of it.

Step 2: Source Answers Our Request and Creates Your Desire

The second step in the process is not our responsibility. Whenever we have a new desire, source energy answers our request immediately. Abraham teaches us that there is a vortex of energy that holds everything we could ever want or imagine, and simply by thinking of a goal, or a wish, we create the equivalent manifestation of that goal in the vortex. We do not need to do anything in order to have our desires fulfilled. They are already fulfilled immediately, as soon as we can think of them. (This is what I was talking about when Jim Carrey said that he knew these wonderful things he wanted are in the making, but just not in his hands yet.)

Step 3: Align with The Vibration of Our Desire

Our job is to align with the energy of that desire. This is the challenging part for most people. To align with our desire, we must put our self into a positive state of emotion, in order to allow the desire to come to us. There is no effort or strain necessary, and in fact, the more we struggle against what we don't want, the harder it is for us to achieve what we do want.

As we learn to relax, trust the process, and flow with the natural current of energy in your life, we will be led, step by step, to the manifestation of what we want. Alignment simply means that you enjoy the process and appreciate the state of not having what we want as much as we appreciate the desire itself. I mentioned that was a challenge for me in my chapter, Law of Attraction... feeling like we had what we wanted, when we don't.

Keep finding things to be grateful for and get into the feeling mode of what it's like to have experienced it already.

Step 4: Maintain Our Alignment Consistently

The first three steps, by themselves, are enough for us to manifest desires. Steps 4 and 5 are about learning to live in a constant state of alignment and connection with our source energy. As we begin to feel the power of alignment and recognize how synchronicity will manifest our desires, the next step in our awareness is to begin to live more consistently from that state.

As we appreciate our desires more fully, and relax into the process of alignment, we will find we will begin to maintain our alignment more consistently and will begin to know quickly whenever we step out of alignment.

Step 5: Appreciate the Contrast

Lastly, Step 5 is the recognition that even our negative experiences are, in some way, supporting our growth and develop. For most people, negative situations trigger negative emotions, but when we truly learn to master our energy this can change. While we will always have new desires and preferences, occasionally we may have complaints, but we will see that even the negative aspects have purpose.

Once I realized this, instead of dwelling on it, I would give a little smile and say to myself, "oh, this is just a little needed contrast." And then I'd let it go as best I could, rather than dwelling.

Chapter Sixteen
Never Too Old

"Nothing shakes the smiling heart."

~ Santosh Kalwar

My eighty-six-year-old friend Beryl will tell you it's a healthy attitude that has kept her living on her farm and playing on a baseball team. That, and to keep moving. She doesn't listen to the societal boundaries placed upon us. She doesn't join her friends on all the ache and pain conversations they seem to like repeating and compete with who is in the worst shape.

I hope our country will continue to shift their paradigm about aging to find more of the beauty that comes with it. I believe we all can find more beauty that can come with aging. I'm happy that I have been able to find some great things about being in my fifties. Not that I think being in the fifties is old, but I thought it was when I was younger.

We need to focus on the positives of aging more, and think about how we see things differently, and often better, then when we were younger. Many people, including myself, were very insecure in our youth. I thought I wasn't super smart or pretty, and I saw a short, chubby girl when I looked in the mirror. Although I was well-liked and even considered popular by some, I didn't feel it. Even in University I lacked much confidence. I wanted to write a romantic fiction novel, but my English Professor didn't think I had the writing talent, and I believed him! It's very unfortunate we are conditioned to believe what the professionals say.

However, the passing of time has greatly changed things for me... thirty plus years later, I probably weigh close to the same as I did in high school; not chubby as I thought I was. Some signs of aging have found their way, but I feel better at 53 than ever! I don't let other opinions hold an ounce of merit, and I did write a book in which did very well... See, there you go Mr. Ross... You just can't squash dreams like that. (Although Bravery was anything but a romantic comedy!)

Experience, confidence and many other great things come with aging. It's so important we know this and discover all that is great about it. It reminds me of an Easter Egg hunt... you can surprise yourself by how much you will find when you put your mind to it. And how wonderful it is when you do. The hunt is as exciting as the find. The journey to the destination is the best; it's the adventure.

A beautiful, kind and lovely friend of mine, Corinna was widowed at a very young age. She was a very happy wife and mom, raising her four-year-old daughter, when her husband died suddenly one day from a heart attack. It was devastating, of course, and led to a life of many challenging years. However, Corinna raised the most beautiful and intelligent daughter.

Now in her mid-fifties, and about a year after her daughter left for university, she began a relationship with a man. She was surprised but delighted to feel the tingle of falling in love again, especially since she wasn't sure she could or would ever love again. It was likely not in the cards after losing her soul mate. Yet now, there was a newfound sparkle in her eye, a skip in her step, and I was so happy for her.

Unfortunately, close to a year later, he betrayed her trust and she was terribly heartbroken. Finally, after all these years she had found love, only to be pulled out from underneath her feet... just like that, everything changed. She was quiet for a few weeks and wanted some time to herself, but she knew I was there for her when she was ready for someone to talk to.

When I talked to her recently, I was in awe of her words. She said, "You know Kim, I'm going to be okay, and I realized for the first time... I am loveable, and I am capable to love again."

I was beyond amazed with her outlook and became full of wonder to the possibilities we have when we look at life this way.

Chapter Seventeen
Dan

"It is a great day anytime I can bring a smile to a girl or boy, knowing that I am helping to inspire them to always dream big."

~ Normani Kordei

When we know what inspires us, if we are fortunate to find what ignites a passion in us, we will have a healthy zest for life. Sadly though, many will go through life without even knowing a true passion for something, and too fearful of change.

Whether it is work, a mentor, a hobby or anything; find something of interest. Our physical and mental wellbeing thrives on joy and satisfaction.

One thing that inspires me is other inspiring people, and recently I made a new friend who exudes a passion and talent for art. Although he has a disability, he never let that stop him from his passion to do what he loves. Every time I think of him, I smile.

His name is Dan Kiplinger and he is a famous artist, among many other talents.

A documentary about him called King Gimp won an Oscar in 2000. But what makes Dan so unique and amazing is how he produces such masterpieces, with the determination to bring them to life and give such meaning to his feelings.

Born with cerebral palsy and very limited motor control, he surpassed all expectations and found his expression through art. Whether it is a sculpture, chalk, or paintbrush on acrylic, there is no conventional way that Dan expresses. When I first viewed some of Dan's paintings I was in awe, but when I saw how he paints, with a paintbrush attached to his forehead, I was astounded. It really is incredible.

Dan's determination to not let his disability define or limit him is fascinating. Becoming a mentor to all those who have challenges, and anyone battling with inadequacy or limitations, his conviction demonstrates we can all live a prosperous and abundant life.

In his own words:

"At first glance, my work addresses my perception of society as a person with a disability. Objects such as my head-stick and my wheelchair are referenced in my artwork as symbols of my everyday obstacles. These pieces, however, are about much more than my disability. I morph and combine these objects with images of my body to create my own vocabulary, which pertains to different life circumstances. Self-perception can be one of the biggest challenges to overcome. No matter how much one explains their situation, we can never fully understand the extent of their individual circumstances, nor think as they do. Obstacles and challenges are a universal part of the human condition. We all face them in everyday life, yet we can choose how we approach them. Many of us are likely to get discouraged during the difficult times in our lives. In my work I hope to encourage viewers to realize that they have the ability to persevere."

For anyone who feels they are stuck in life, or at a crossroad of some sort, whether you are typical or special needs, I highly recommend you watch Dan's documentary, King Gimp. I'm sure it will bring a new clarity, and possibly change your perspective on life.

When I first talked to Dan and learned about all his great accomplishments, I felt like the sky is the limit to what us humans are capable of. When we place limitations on our abilities because of what the typical societal norm is, then we will never reach our full potential.

Thanks, Dan, for sharing your gifts with us and demonstrating that despite your struggles, life can be wonderful.... it's our future to decide.
Here is a great link of Dan's to check out:
https://www.youtube.com/watch?v=1mvP69g_Oak

Get inspired, learn from adversity... take our experiences and give them a purpose. We can make a positive difference in our life as well as those we know. As I love to say; it's never too late!

Chapter Eighteen
Spin it Around

"Life is like a mirror. Smile at it and it smiles back at you."
~ Peace Pilgrim

D o you know that we don't have to change one single thing in our life in order to bring more positivity in? Yes, that's right. All we must do is think differently about it.

Let me explain.

Each of us are separate individuals who interpret life, circumstances, events, etc., in our own unique way. How wonderful... no one can tell us, or make us interpret something their way, no matter how hard they try, if we don't want to. Depending on where we are, and our position in life, there may be people telling us to do things every day. Our managers tell us what we need to do at work... parents tell their children to do their chores... the law tells us what we need to obey. The traffic light tells us when to stop, when to go, and the list goes on. Our world is full of people and things telling us what to do all day long. But the one thing no one can tell us to do is how to think or how to feel. It's a beautiful wondrous gift. Our thoughts, our interpretations are all uniquely our own, and how we choose to use them is up to us. So, think about spinning in a more positive direction, if you are not already doing so.

Just like this:

You may think what a crummy job I have as a janitor, and how mundane it is to clean up other people's messes all day, but how about thinking; what a great and prideful responsibility it is to provide a cleaner and healthier environment for all I service.

You may think what a depressing job it is to work in a graveyard, but you could also view it as a wonderful opportunity to be able to work outdoors and provide a beautiful surrounding for someone's final resting place.

Every aspect of life has a different outlook, it just depends on how we want to see it. Awareness is one of our biggest freedoms, and opportunities to 'spin it around.'

Here is one example of my own. It's not a huge revelation, but it's interesting to demonstrate even the little things that we can accomplish by turning the frequency dial of our thoughts.

As well, starting with little endeavors paves the way to succeed with bigger ones.

I used to have a strong dislike for vacuuming, but because I have so many animals, I vacuum every day. However, I would always procrastinate because I dread doing it, and that just prolongs the agony. One day I thought, 'Okay Kim, you are going to have to vacuum approximately 200 more hours this year, so how can you possibly change your attitude about hating to vacuum?' I thought about it for a bit, and it wasn't long before I figured out an answer. I changed my mindset. I focused on the feeling of how good it feels to be done, and how gratifying to have such a clean house. I also thought how fortunate I was to have a vacuum cleaner. Many people in the world, especially third world countries, don't even have a vacuum. It sounds simple but it works. I don't love vacuuming, but I don't mind doing it at all anymore. I put in my ear buds to listen to motivational stuff, or some of my favorite music. (Great example of The Law of Attraction.)

Recently my girlfriend had a 1,000-pound granite blade saw fall on her leg. Thankfully, she was okay, but had two sprains and a very banged up bruised leg. Prior to this she had been going through a lot of turmoil in her life, and I was a little worried about her state of mind, until I talked to her. I was kind of expecting to hear, 'well it just figures something like this would happen,' or 'What next?' Often, when a string of negative events happens, we adopt this attitude. But nope, not Denise. She said, "I was just lucky that it wasn't worse, or that it wasn't my dad, who was beside me."

Her feelings could have gone in the opposite direction very easily and almost expectantly, but what a great way to 'spin it around.'

If you find yourself in a position where some aspects of your life may be bringing you down, just try looking for another way of thinking about it... you never know until you try, and your findings may surprise you. Another beautiful thing about our lives is that it is never too late to change our outlook.

The only limitations we have are the ones we put on ourselves, and beauty is in the eye of the beholder.

Chapter Nineteen
Share the Love

"A warm smile is the universal language of kindness."
~ William Arthur Ward

Y ou probably have heard this expression, and my Grandma used to say it to us grandchildren all the time, "If you can't say anything nice, then don't say anything at all." As you recall from earlier chapters, to me she was the most remarkable and wise woman.

At the time, I didn't think much of it, but as I grew, I would begin to understand more and more, why she said that. I saw kids get bullied, including myself, I saw adults bully other adults, and demean their self-esteem. As an adult now, I still see this, and even more so. I see politician's slagging each other, road rage, derogatory rants on Social Media... hate, hate, and more hate. We must smarten up.

We are one, and you'd think with the Covid-19 pandemic collectively affecting the entire world, we would see this. Maybe we will. We better, if we still want to live in a sustainable world. Perhaps it will take the sacrifice of all those who die and the pain of the frontline workers, to see we need to come together. But I see each country, each state, each city practicing very different measures.

As I'm writing this book, I received a message from my work colleague, Dr. Soni. He sent me a video of a woman reading a famous letter that Albert Einstein wrote to his daughter. I was fascinated by the fact that it came with the timing it did. It has been floating in the ether for all those years, but lands in my lap as I'm writing this book which follows the principles of this chapter. It was a goosebumps moment, and I hope it enters and touches your life in the same perfect time as it did mine.

In the late 1980s, the daughter of the famous genius, donated 1,400 letters, written by Einstein, to the Hebrew University, with orders not to publish their contents until two decades after his death.

Here is one of them:

"When I proposed the theory of relativity, very few understood me, and what I will reveal now to transmit to mankind will also collide with the misunderstanding and prejudice in the world. I ask you to guard the letters if necessary, years, decades, until society is advanced enough to accept what I will explain below.

There is an extremely powerful force that, so far, science has not found a formal explanation to. It is a force that includes and governs all others and is even behind any phenomenon operating in the universe and has not yet been identified by us.

This universal force is LOVE.

When scientists looked for a unified theory of the universe, they forgot the most powerful unseen force.

Love is Light, that enlightens those who give and receive it. Love is gravity, because it makes some people feel attracted to others.

Love is power, because it multiplies the best we have, and allows humanity not to be extinguished in their blind selfishness. Love unfolds and reveals.

For love we live and die.

Love is God and God is Love.

This force explains everything and gives meaning to life. This is the variable that we have ignored for too long, maybe because we are afraid of love because it is the only energy in the universe that man has not learned to drive at will.

To give visibility to love, I made a simple substitution in my most famous equation.

If instead of $E = mc2$, we accept that the energy to heal the world can be obtained through love multiplied by the speed of light squared, we arrive at the conclusion that love is the most powerful force there is, because it has no limits.

After the failure of humanity in the use and control of the other forces of the universe that have turned against us, it is urgent that we nourish ourselves with another kind of energy.

If we want our species to survive, if we are to find meaning in life, if we want to save the world and every sentient being that inhabits it, love is the one and only answer.

Perhaps we are not yet ready to make a bomb of love, a device powerful enough to destroy the hate, selfishness and greed that devastate the planet.
However, each individual carry within them a small but powerful generator of love whose energy is waiting to be released.

When we learn to give and receive this universal energy, dear Lieserl, we will have affirmed that love conquers all, is able to transcend everything and anything, because love is the quintessence of life.

I deeply regret not having been able to express what is in my heart, which has quietly beaten for you all my life. Maybe it's too late to apologize, but as time is relative, I need to tell you that I love you and thanks to you I have reached the ultimate answer!"

Your father
Albert Einstein

Isn't this so fascinating and true! It's simple to practice... we just need to use our outside voice for good and not evil. There is a dispute as to the authenticity of Einstein being the author, but that's not the point. The power is behind the meaning, no matter who the author.

We are all one, as best interpreted in my favorite line from Shakespeare:
"If you prick us, do we not bleed? if you tickle us, do we not laugh? if you poison us, do we not die? and if you wrong us, shall we not revenge?" - (Act III, scene I)

It's a good reminder that we are all made of the same cloth. And anything is possible, once we become aware.

I'm hoping these trying times will remind us how important it is to share the love because that is how we will best recover. Share it in any manner you see fit. Share with those who need what you can give. Whether it's your food, time, clothes, money or love... share what you have.

Chapter Twenty
Be More Aware

"What sunshine is to flowers; smiles are to humanity."

~ Joseph Addison

That same sentence my grandma would say, "If you can't say anything nice, then don't say anything at all," also reminds me of our 'inside vs. outside' voices. Not only did it make me think how many people say things they shouldn't, it made me think of the things we should say and don't.

I'm guilty of this regarding my husband. Sometimes I take him for granted and don't show my appreciation as much as I should. I spend a lot of time lifting others but sometimes forget about my own family. But now that I'm aware of this, I can change. How wonderful is that!

Yesterday was Sunday, and Cam spent all day landscaping in the backyard. Digging up sod, and probably 30 trips or more wheelbarrows of rock transported. He worked tirelessly and was completely exhausted at the end of the day. He asked what I thought, and I told him everything was coming together nicely, and how good it will look when it's all done. Well okay, not a negative remark in any way, but perhaps a little undeserving of the 'blood, sweat and tears' he shed that day. So today I text him a message saying how I was enjoying my morning coffee in the backyard and how beautiful it was. I said thank you so much for all your hard work yesterday, I really appreciate it! Now, that was much better, don't you think?

'Treat others as we wish to be treated.' It's just that simple.

Give back when we can... whether it is volunteering our time, donating clothes, food, or money, there is always something we can do to support each other. We will reap some lovely benefits in return. I particularly like the Do-Good Live Well study from 2010. It's data which is very similar to other studies and shows:

Of those who volunteered, 68 percent reported that it made them feel physically healthier; 89 percent had improvement in self being (e.g., happiness); and 73 percent had lowered stress levels.

I've heard some people say giving to others is a kind of a selfish act because it makes us feel better about ourselves. Which if there is anything good to come from being selfish, I guess that would be it. However, when we are giving while inadvertently receiving joy and satisfaction from it, it is a win. The typical selfish person only thinks of themself.

When you think about any selfish, unkind people you know, I will bet you find they have mostly grumpy, cynical dispositions who generally like to put down others or find fault. You probably also know some wonderful giving people who are likely always positive and happy.

Kind people are compassionate people. You can't have one without the other. There will be times in our life where compassion from someone will save us. You may already know this because someone's compassion saved you. So, every time you see an opportunity to show some, take it!

Compliment. When you notice a family member, friend or acquaintance is looking particularly lovely, give them a nice compliment. You will possibly make their day. Try it and watch their whole-body language change, and a smile emerge. Some people are shy and don't take a compliment very well and probably blush a little, but that's okay, you will have none the less made them feel good. It may be the only time they smile that day.

Do you ever think something nice about someone when you see them, but don't say anything? I have, and then wonder after, 'why didn't I tell them how nice they looked today?' Now that I am aware, I try to use my 'outside voice' more often. Even just noticing little things about others, like a new hairdo, or how proud of them you are for all their volunteer work. It's easy to find something nice to say, but make sure you are authentic.

After I got off the phone with my friend Denise, who I talked about in the last chapter, I texted her to say how proud I was of her attitude to remain positive in an imperfect time. I had realized I was thinking it, and saying it in my inside voice, but she's not a mind reader!

Try it yourself; you'll probably see how you use your inside voice more often than you think. Take note of how you feel when you do or say something nice and notice how it will bring a smile to your face too.

Chapter Twenty-One
Gratitude

"Don't cry because it's over. Smile because it happened."
~ Dr. Suess

April 11, 2020. Listening to the news this morning is part encouraging and part disheartening. Some countries are flattening the curve and collectively coming together while others are getting worse, but we must get on the same page to eradicate this worldwide virus and get back on our feet. It seems like most politicians want to pass blame and point fingers.

We are all affected in some way, and unfortunately too many people have lost love one's. We're losing jobs, some will lose their business and homes. We are in a crisis and all around is devastation, confusion, and very sad stories. In parts of the world, essential workers are exhausted and many feeling defeated. People are dying all over the world, and most by themselves; no one to comfort them or hold their hand.

Our future is uncertain because it's challenging to see a light at the end of the tunnel. It's daunting to think about what we have ahead of us, and what it will take to rise above. But the best thing to do is not think about the challenges that lay ahead. Instead think of the tasks at hand, and what we can do now.

I try to find anything I can to be grateful for in these uncertain times. We must because a stronger spirit will prevail over a sick one. I'm grateful for all the people who are coming together to help, whether it is making masks from home, preparing meals for the poor, or checking on the lonely and vulnerable. I'm so appreciative for all the front line and essential employees, and those who show patronage to them.

It's difficult to be positive in times like this, but if we can find a little somewhere, it will make difference. Worry is counterproductive, but I know, easier said than done to eradicate. I find myself worrying about Avery. Although he is healthy, the virus can attack the heart. When I find my mind wandering to fear, I nip it in the bud and say to myself, 'Kim, stay in the present. Right now, Avery is healthy and home with you.' This helps when I catch it in time before the thought gets carried away.

I hear it all the time, 'we are all in this together,' which brings some comfort to know we are not alone. During this surreal time, I am amazed at how many people are staying positive and finding gratitude. It was great to see comments after I posted a question asking what positives people have discovered during this time.

Here are a few:

» Lori Ambrosetti — I've had the best conversations with my kids. I'm grateful for a roof over my head and fridge full of food.

» Heather Johnston Bier — I learned that what we have is enough and all the excess is not necessary! It's fun to have but we really don't need it.

» Victoria Jackson — I am so thankful Bill is working from home now and has designated himself as our family shopper, because I am immune compromised. We are blessed to enjoy each other's company, and we love cocooning anyway with each other and our pets. There are always wonderful books to read, cooking to enjoy, crafts to make, games to play, movies to watch. We are blessed in so many ways!

» Liana Snippa — I am thankful to have the opportunity to be home where I can make beautiful dinners every night and have great conversations with my son without being hurried. I can catch up on all the projects I have around the home and enjoy doing them. I am happy to catch up on my paperwork. I've been using this time wisely and using up everything in my freezer. LOL. Not working and Interacting with my friends and clients that I love is hard but there's so much at home to do and to love. I will embrace my time.

» Deborah Murrin — I am learning that it is ok to be still. It is ok to not do everything and enjoy the quiet moments. It is also ok to not go shopping as much.

» Carol Marleau — The home truly is where the heart is.

» Shawn Mclean — I have really understood the importance of family and friends; not that I didn't know before, but this is something no one has ever dealt with. I can't wait until I can see loved ones and family. I have been calling people more than ever before and reconnecting.

These are just a few of many. They all have similarities which reflect love and a strength to overcome. There wasn't one negative response.

Just look at our power to shine in the darkest of days.

I can identify with all the above, and to add one thing that I've been appreciative to learn is my ability to use the food items in my cupboards very creatively. Last night I made the best left-over mashed potato casserole with corn, mushrooms, eggs, green onions, cheese and sour cream. (I have the recipe if anyone wants it.) I love that I have learned to use all I have and not waste anything.

This extra time has also allowed me to try new things for the first time in my life and it was kind of funny because I clearly wasn't using the proper tools that I needed. My neighbor saw me struggling with the weeding and brought over a few funny looking utensils and demonstrated how they work. (Social distancing or course.) I was so grateful. It must have saved at least a couple hours of time, and much frustration. What's wonderful about gratitude is when we provide it, we also receive it.

Let's stand up, lets speak up, lets reach out to each other.

Smile Again

Chapter Twenty-Two
In Times of Trouble

"Your smile will give you a positive countenance that will make people feel comfortable around you."

~ Les Brown

N ow more than ever, we need to support our vulnerable. Self-isolating and what will be our new normal could be detrimental to many of our young, introverted, or mental health populations. Processing and adapting to change come much harder than our typical population. It is something we really need to bring to the forefront, and we need to do better.

If you have young or special needs people in your network of family and friends, be especially aware of any changes in actions or behaviors. Stressful times elevate anxiety for many people, especially those with special needs, so we need to take extra precautions.

Be alert for the bully mentality that targets the vulnerable population. In haphazard times, fear instigates the bullies even more. We need to know what to look for, and we all need to educate ourselves better on the signs of bully's and the bullied... we can never know too much about it. It's a good idea to Google information sites on bullying to learn more because it comes in all different shapes and sizes, affecting us at any age. Although we'd like to think we've made progress, we have a long way to go. We must learn some tools to stop bullying.

Jesse was bullied in school, but fortunately her close friends told me, and I was able to meet with the principal, along with the bullying student and his parents to put an end to it.

When I first heard this was happening, of course I was furious and wanted revenge. The mama bear emerged with a vengeance. However, my level head prevailed when I remembered a greatly repeated phrase growing up, 'two wrongs don't make a right.'

We were fortunate to have friends that spoke up, but many victims will not. I later found out that the boy that bullied Jesse was also a victim of bullying.

Adults are certainly not immune to bullying either, and is prevalent in elderly environments. Anyone who is vulnerable is at a higher risk to be a bully's target. Although society has been advocating anti bullying much more in the past decade, it still exists at alarming rates. Here are some statistics:

More than one out of every five (20.8%) students report being bullied (National Center for Educational Statistics, 2016).

The federal government began collecting data on school bullying in 2005, when the prevalence of bullying was around 28 percent (Department of Education, 2015).

Rates of bullying vary across studies (from 9% to 98%). A meta-analysis of 80 studies analyzing bullying involvement rates (for both bullying others and being bullied) for 12-18-year-old students reported a mean prevalence rate of 35% for traditional bullying involvement and 15% for cyberbullying involvement (Middeck, Minchin, Harbaugh, Guerra, & Runions, 2014).

33% of students who reported being bullied at school indicated that they were bullied at least once or twice a month during the school year (National Center for Educational Statistics, 2016).

Of those students who reported being bullied, 13% were made fun of, called names, or insulted; 12% were the subject of rumors; 5% were pushed, shoved, tripped, or spit on; and 5%

were excluded from activities on purpose (National Center for Educational Statistics, 2016).

A slightly higher portion of female than of male student's report being bullied at school (23% vs. 19%). In contrast, a higher percentage of male than of female student's report being physically bullied (6% vs. 4%) and threatened with harm (5% vs. 3%; (National Center for Educational Statistics, 2016).

Bullied students reported that bullying occurred in the following places: the hallway or stairwell at school (42%), inside the classroom (34%), in the cafeteria (22%), outside on school grounds (19%), on the school bus (10%), and in the bathroom or locker room (9%) (National Center for Educational Statistics, 2016).

43% of bullied students report notifying an adult at school about the incident. Students who report higher rates of bullying victimization are more likely to report the bullying (National Center for Educational Statistics, 2016).
More than half of bullying situations (57%) stop when a peer intervenes on behalf of the student being bullied (Hawkins, Pepler, & Craig, 2001).

School-based bullying prevention programs decrease bullying by up to 25% (McCallion & Feder, 2013).

The reasons for being bullied reported most often by students include physical appearance, race/ethnicity, gender, disability, religion, sexual orientation (National Center for Educational Statistics, 2016).

I know the people who pick up this book are not the bullying type, but we don't have to be a bully to stop bullying. We can be aware citizens who look out for each other, protect and support. This pandemic has increased hate crimes and discrimination, and awareness is the first factor to begin repair.

Let's ammo up people and make a positive difference in someone's life so they too can 'smile again.'

Change starts with us, and it can start today.

Smile Again

Chapter Twenty-Three
We'll Learn the Hard Way

"The real man smiles in trouble, gathers strength from distress, and grows brave by reflection."

~ Thomas Paine

Global warming, nuclear war threats, disease and over population, are just a few recipes of disaster knocking on earth's door. Will the Coronavirus pandemic be the trigger to make the difference we desperately need to see for this world to be healthy again?

Well if it is, it's certainly not the way we would want to learn the lesson. But when you think about it how could there have been any other way? A tragedy of this proportion gives us all a wakeup call to help us realize we are all connected.

For the sake of all those who have lost their life, or those who have suffered greatly, I hope the sacrifices you made will be the purpose to see the change our world needs.

It appears when we can give purpose to tragedy, then it wasn't all for nothing.

Many people believe this pandemic will be equivalent to the economic downfall of The Great Depression over one hundred years ago. Maybe every hundred years we need to be reminded of our shortcomings. Although we can't change what we have created, we can focus on the silver lining it can bring if we are smart, and heed what may be the most important lesson of our life.

I only knew a little about The Great Depression, but what I did know came from my grandma who lived through it. What I gathered and wish to share today is what I hope is a comparison of how we will proceed.

My Grandpa and Grandma bought land after the depression because they said if it ever happens again, we will have land to raise livestock and soil to grow food.

That land was passed on to Mom and her siblings, which they still own today.

Wisdom was learned the hard way when the financial crash put families in such an awful situation. It's heartbreaking to think back on how hard they struggled just to survive — but on the opposite end of the spectrum, their resilience was inspiring.

When I did a little research, it was interesting to see some of the silver linings following such a horrific time.

Here are some valued lessons from the Great Depression that made a lasting impression on the generations that followed it.

~ Never Use Something Just Once

"Disposable" wasn't part of many people's vocabulary during the Depression. Even scraps could be sewed together and made into something new. Nothing was ever wasted. I find myself doing this with food since our visits to the grocery store are limited. And some people in our house, no names mentioned, have learned how to not waste toilet paper!

~ Learn More Than One Trade

There was no such thing as job security, so being able to adapt to different fields wherever they could find work was essential.

~ Make Friends with Your Neighbors

Communities rallied together to keep every mouth fed — and to support each other through the emotional pain that often came with trying to make ends meet, according to historians.

~ You Might Have to Get Your Hands Dirty

In fact, a lot people didn't even have a choice. Most families grew their own groceries right in their backyard and became innovative to utilize every available space they had.

~ Don't Put All Your Eggs in One Basket

The lesson we've all thankfully embraced in more modern times of diversifying your funds was at the core of the whole Depression. That, and to save a hefty stash of tangible cash to keep around just in case.

~ Learn the Difference Between Want and Need

There's obviously an emphasis on material things and high-tech gadgets today that everybody wants... but do we really need? However, during the Depression, even when things seemed to be at their worst, communities still found ways to entertain themselves with simple (and inexpensive) fun. I think this is happening for many of us now. Board games were vastly a thing of the past until recently.

~ Always Keep A Sharp Eye for Good Deals

While out using what little money they had, they made sure to use it right by never settling for the first option. Being savvy with coupons, haggling, and other ways to stretch their pennies kept families from going without for too long.

~ Protect Your Family at All Costs

According to the Encyclopedia, crime rates went through the roof during the Depression. Headlines were filled with stories ranging from bootleggers attempting to skirt the Prohibition laws and outlaws like Bonnie and Clyde making their way across the country robbing any cash register they could get their hands on. Families relied on each other to remain safe and protected, making the bonds between them more important.

~ It's Okay to Embrace Little Escapes

According to CBS News, who spoke with a man who was living during the era, people found catharsis in the fictional stories playing at movie theaters. Classic films like 'The Wizard of Oz' helped them forget about their own troubles and dip their toes into a fantasy world for at least a few hours. Now with technology advancements and having to social distance, we are fortunate to be able to watch the classics in the comfort of our own home.

~ Get Creative to Keep Your Cupboards Full

You don't see many folks canning and preserving food these days, but it was at its peak when the cupboards were in danger of going completely bare throughout the Depression. It might be a good idea for this to make a comeback with more families today. My mom still cans, and probably has enough reserve to live on for a few months.

~ Remember to Focus on What Really Matters

Above all the hardships that were thrown their way, one of the most important, if not the most, things that helped people find the strength to carry on: love. Families spent more time together, with every member doing whatever they could to keep a smile on everyone's face. Post-Covid will bring back some of these basic principles that got lost in our economies hunger for power and growth.

I wish it didn't take great tragedies and sacrifices to make the change we need to see, but it seems that's the only way we can hear the worlds cries.

Chapter Twenty-Four
When We're Ready, It Will Come

"A simple smile. That's the start of opening your heart and being compassionate to others."

~ Dalai Lama

When you have the time, watch the movie 'Field of Dreams' starring Kevin Costner. 'If you build it, they will come.' Although it's fiction, it's a relatable analogy of how good things come easier when we are ready and prepared.

When we know what we want, we are far more likely to receive it because we have aligned our frequency to the receiving mode. As Abraham Hicks says, 'We have to be tuned in, tapped in and turned on.'

It was approximately 2006 when my girlfriend Cheryl gave me a Law of Attraction video to watch. She said, "Kim, you gotta watch this video; it's all about how thoughts become things and we can get what we ask for, and our mindsets determine our happiness and fulfillment." She was so excited and did her best to sell me. However, for some reason, I never watched the video. Every month or so she would ask me if I have watched it yet, and I would say no, but I will. I didn't think about it at the time, but I wasn't ready.

She ended up taking the video back to lend it to someone else. Months later, I came across a YouTube link called 'The Strangest Secret' by Earl Nightingale, recorded in 1956. It was all about The Law of Attraction, creating our own destinies and reaching our height of happiness through a new understanding of thought process. I absorbed every word and was fascinated and excited about this new revelation.

Because I was willing and ready, I began to adopt a new state of being. There is something unique about the Universe in the way it only gives you certain things when you are ready to receive them. If you think about it, you can probably come up with some examples of your own.

When I first began to feel the abundance from utilizing the philosophies from The Law of Attraction, I was so excited and talked to everyone about it. However, people weren't responding the way they were supposed to, or in the way I thought they should respond. Could they not see the how great this is?

Then it dawned on me, they were like me when my girlfriend Cheryl was so excited to share her experience with me. They weren't ready for receiving something new, and maybe they didn't want to change their beliefs. I was not their inspiration for change at that time, and you can't change that.

One of those people was my husband, Cam. This was a source of frustration at first. We all want people to be on board when we are so freshly excited about something! But I had to accept that I can't make someone change their beliefs. Staying frustrated about it only makes it worse. Cam would always say things like, "We don't make enough money," or "No, we can't afford it." Ughh! ... that was like fingernails on the chalk board!! 'Don't say that! You'll never be able to afford anything with that attitude. Don't you know the rich get richer and the poor get poorer because if you always do what you've always done, you'll always get what you already have.'

Change our mindset and the whole game changes.

Slowly Cam started to see the positive changes in me and naturally adopted a similar mind set. I'm even rubbing off a bit on my mom. She used to say, "I always pick the longest line ups at the grocery store," or "I can never find a good parking spot." It's funny because that's exactly what I used to say, and that's what I would always get. But now, you can guess, I always get fabulous parking spots and shortest line ups. Occasionally I won't, and I get a little surprised, but then I smile and say, 'A bit of contrast is good.'

Another great analogy was when I bought Eckhart Tolle's book, A New Earth, many years ago, and way before I read his book, The Power of Now. I had heard about Eckhart Tolle, and the popularity of his well-received spiritual teachings, and was excited to 'dig my nose in.' However, once I started reading, I quickly became confused. I was having to reread every sentence multiple times because nothing was sinking in. It was like reading a language I didn't understand. I kept trying and trying, but there was no use. So off in a box it went. About 7 years later, I found it in a drawer I was cleaning out. (Yes, I know, I should clean out my drawers more often.) Anyway, I picked it up and remembered my attempts to read it years earlier, and how I couldn't make any sense of it. I wondered if this time things might be different. After all, much time had passed since then, and I was more educated about The Law of Attraction and related spiritual teachings. It wasn't a coincidence I kept the book and found it all these years later. This time I was ready to understand and embrace the wealth of information Eckhart shared.

I enjoyed all it offered, and it felt so liberating to see how we can open up a closed mind. Many people don't like change, or rather think they don't. I believe it's not change they don't like, it's their fear that stops the opportunity for change.

Smile Again

Chapter Twenty-Five
Contrast

"If the world's a veil of tears, smile till rainbows span it."

~ Lucy Larcom

S peaking of contrast, we all know there will be dark times in our lives. Experiences and circumstances happen that we can't predict or change. Pandemics, disease, broken relationships, and many other circumstances are some hurdles that we will all encounter at some point. But, as earlier mentioned; how we deal with it is our choice. And experiencing challenging times helps us to value and appreciate the wonderful ones much greater. I know I am more of a grateful mom after living through the months of Avery's heart surgeries and near deaths.

We naturally value life more once we have seen the threat of it taken away. The most trying times are losing our loved ones. The pain can be so great that it is hard to, and too difficult to carry on for a spell. But once some healing can begin, we hope to come to understand, 'It's better to have loved and lost, than to never have love at all.' Although my dearest Dad and Grandmother are in Heaven, I think and dream of them often. Their wisdom lives in me, and they are still here with me spiritually. The healing has taken place, but the scar will forever remain. A part of us leaves with our loved ones.

I recently had to put down our beloved pet, Mya. Being a huge animal lover, this was a terrible time for me. Mya was my four-pound Chihuahua and came everywhere with me. Even shopping I would put her in my purse. It's so hilarious because every picture of me at home has Mya photo bombing me in the background. Every night she slept above my head on my pillow. She could always sense if I was going to be going somewhere, and park herself by the door so I wouldn't miss taking her with me. I spent way more time with her than my husband or children.

I knew her health was failing due to an enlarged heart, but with medication our vet said it was difficult to say how much time we had left with her. I knew she was on borrowed time, but you are never prepared to say good-bye.

On her last day we drove up the hill to our favorite walking spot. I could tell she was more listless because normally she can't wait to get out the door, but on this morning, she just looked at me.

I picked her up thinking a walk would perk her up, but sadly no... she took a few steps and laid down. Her panting and labored breathing began to escalate, and I just knew this would be our last trip up the mountain.

I began to sob uncontrollably as I picked her up and held her in my arms. She seemed more content with me holding her, so I did our usual route carrying her. Tears streamed down as I feared this would be our last walk together, and it was.

After arriving to the vets, my fear was confirmed. The vet said her lungs were filled with fluid and her little heart has given up. After eleven years, it was Mya's time to rest in peace. I was a mess, and our whole family was too. I walked around completely vacant for days, feeling so lonely not having my sidekick beside me. The doorbell rings and there's no barking. My hand lifts above my head on the pillow in the middle of the night, and there is no Mya there to comfort me. That welcoming smile and wagging tail at the end of a stressful day is gone. Walks and bike rides are empty and lonely, and everyone asks where Mya is. Life is not the same without my little sidekick.

In time, the tears will get fewer and further in between, and smiles will slowly replace tears as wonderful memories allow us to adjust to her absence.

My mom says she has loved and lost too many animals and that is why she will never get another one. I get that... I have lost many of my cats and dogs that I loved dearly. For now, I still believe it is better to have loved and lost, than to never have loved at all. But perhaps we can get to a point when we say, "I've lost too many and I just can't do it anymore."

You never get used to it, and you can never get prepared for it.

I can't think about getting another dog right now... the pain of losing Mya is too raw right now. However, thankfully most of us humans have this wondrous gift to eventually dull out the pain and fondly remember the fun times we spent together. I thank God for the ability to know time heals our wounds.

Scars may remain, but if we look at it in a positive light... those scars can be a reminder to live in the moment and enjoy the time we have with our loved ones, and fondly remember the ones who once were.

Tomorrow isn't promised to anyone, so let's make the best of everyday and everyone.

* This chapter was a blog I wrote over a couple of years ago and thought it would be a good chapter for this book.

Over a year later we have since got a new dog, Murphy. A local rescue company posted a picture of him after they got him from California. He was found in rough shape on the streets. Cam showed me his picture and I knew we had to have him. Ohhhhh, he had a face only a mother could love. We are not sure what kind of dog he is, perhaps some Terrier and Chihuahua. People always grin when we walk by, and many ask what kind of dog he is because he looks so unusual. He's about 15 – 20 pounds, a white and orange face that looks like a grumpy old man, and a piggy nose, with floppy orange ears. He doesn't look that threatening but he is quite protective of our family because he knows we saved him

He hasn't taken Mya's place, and is unlike her in many ways, but he is my new sidekick now and I love him.

Smile Again

Chapter Twenty-Six
Mentors

"There is little success where there is little laughter."

~ Andrew Carnegie

O ur world wouldn't be near as advanced without mentors. We learn from their lead. Mentors give us inspiration, motivation and desire to improve. Everyone should have at least one mentor. I am fortunate to have many. A mentor doesn't have to have a lot of fame or make large worldly contributions. They can be everyday people who lead a wonderful example, even family members too.

My mom was only fifty-six when my dad died, and they had been together since she was Fourteen. Most of her entire life was with my dad and now he was gone. Mom's daily life was remote, working at home on the horse farm, and bookkeeper for Dad's trucking business. She didn't have a lot of outside contact other than with friends and family. Now her entire way of life is taken from her, but for some reason I didn't worry about her as much as one would think under the circumstances. Of course, she is heartbroken, but I just knew she was a strong woman who would be okay.

Although she had never mowed a lawn in her life because Dad had to have the perfect checker design, Mom learned how to maneuver the big ride-on lawn mower to recreate Dad's pattern. She also learned how to fix fan belts, patch roofs, and anything else that needed being done around the house, without one complaint. I have so much admiration for her courage and strength. She is very smart and beautiful, so you could imagine all the men coming 'out of the woodwork' to ask her out after Dad passed. But no, she was an independent woman, happy on her own, and now almost twenty-two years later, she is still going strong!

Many years ago, Cam brought me home a book called Choosing to Smile, (which I didn't even correlate when naming Smile Again.) Cam said, "I bought this for you. The authors all live here in Chilliwack, and I thought you'd like to read it."

It was about three woman who collaborated to write their story about beating cancer, and all three pretty ladies were posed together for the book cover. I thought it was neat to have local authors who live in our town. After all, I always wanted to write a book.

I was impressed with these ladies' stories of courage, and especially with Glenda's. It was the most inspiring adventure about her brave fight to beat cancer. When I mean brave, I mean completely fearless. When I think about brave people and their stories, I always think back to the part in Glenda's book where she had to make a life altering decision to have her leg amputated.

She said to the doctor immediately after being faced with the choice, "cut it off." The doctor said, "I'm not so sure you understood what I said." She said, "Yes I understood, cut it off."

It was a smart decision to take the risk of any advancement of her bone cancer, and Glenda not only survived but she became a mother, grandmother, one of the most outstanding authors, philanthropists, and motivational speakers She would also be awarded The Caring Canadian Award, The Diamond Jubilee, among many others. To me she became my biggest motivator. Glenda inspired me to begin to write Bravery. Although it took a few years to complete, it was the most satisfying, gratifying accomplishment for me!

One day, I was feeling adventurous and Googled Glenda's name, and pleasantly surprised to find her email address. I was so excited to send her an email to thank her for all her service and for being an inspiring mentor to me. I told her I finished my book and would send her a copy once it was published. I also asked her if she knew my grandma since Grandma would provide support and give visits to anyone who lost a limb. I couldn't believe my eyes when the very next day I received a reply!

She said she had heard of my grandma, Gwen McKay, but she had passed before Glenda lost her leg. She also asked if I had an editor and offered to proofread my manuscript! Even thinking about it brings back the excitement I felt. And then, I couldn't believe it when I found out she just lived around the corner from me!

Going to her house was very exciting; I felt like I was meeting a famous movie star. Glenda greeted me at the door with the most beautiful smile of welcome and warmth. I don't recall seeing eyes that sparkle with such kindness before. She gave me a big hug and we went inside for coffee and had the loveliest visit.

Its uncanny how both my grandma and Glenda lost their legs, and both would go on to serve others and help all those in need.

Glenda and I became great friends, and I was so honored for her shining endorsement on Bravery's book cover.

When we have mentors, we have guidance, and we all need a little of that from time to time.

Smile Again

Chapter Twenty-Seven
Be Careful What You Wish For

"Before you put on a frown, make absolutely sure there are no smiles available."

~ Jim Beggs

Before any great improvements, or the manifestations of our desires are set in motion, it is very important we are certain of what that looks like, and how it will affect our life going forward. Is what you want, what you really want? We may feel we have a clear idea of what we want, but if we don't consider how our lives will change when we get it, we could end up less happy than when we started.

I heard of a person that yearned for the day they could retire. It's all he ever talked about, even fifteen or more years before it was his time. Without realizing it, he was shortcoming himself from life's journey. When we are too busy focusing on our desires, we don't pay attention to all we have to be grateful for now. We pull out of the important practice of living in the present.

When retirement finally came, this person was not happy at all. He never realized that he would be too old to do a lot of the things he wanted. Age had diminished his energy and stamina. Some of the friends he wanted to spend more time with had passed away, and so had his parents. His children were grown and moved away. He was angry because he realized he screwed up. He missed enjoying and appreciating all he had because he was too focused on what he thought he wanted.

I'm sure you have your own examples of people you know, or even yourself, when you got something you wished for, only to realize it didn't bring with it the greatness you thought.

I remember wanting to move out of our small town and into the big city so bad. I wanted to have a prestigious job, make lots of money and wear expensive clothes. This was my definition of success at the time. Thankfully not anymore, but back then, that was what I thought was my recipe for happiness.

So, I moved to Vancouver, got a job with a promotions company making good money and moved to Ontario to make even more money. Well, I was miserable! I missed my family and friends so much and my grandma died while I was there.

I think I lasted only a few months before I moved back. What a reality check that was for me, but a good learning lesson.

If we aren't careful, getting what we think we want could be a recipe for disaster. There is a delicate balance. That's why I talked earlier about finding little things to be grateful for every day. Yes, it's great to have desires and aspirations, if they don't consume us, or inhibit our current contentment for living in the now.

Sometimes we are not often happier when we obtain things on our wish list, that's why it's important to be happy now. Happiness is an inside job. A smile is displayed on the outside, but it is made from the inside. Objects, or things are not going to make us happy for the long term.

A popular universal want is to win the lotto. Many people believe this would make them the happiest person on earth, but in fact, many who win lotto's have learned otherwise. Everyone wants to be their friend; who do you trust? Some lotto winners are not educated on investing and saving, so they end up losing more than what they had in the first place! Research shows that most lotto winners will lose their winnings within seven years.

Getting excited about our desires coming true is healthy, but we must be clear that getting what we want is not a guaranteed solution or provider of eternal happiness. We aren't going to reach some utopian state of bliss once our desires manifest. If happiness is what we're after, and most of the time it is, we're wise to focus on how we can cultivate it right here and now, before we've bought the yacht, the house in Hawaii, or won the lotto. Life is always happening in the present moment, so it's important for us to realize that while we wish, want and dream, our real lives are taking place right now!

Chapter Twenty-Eight
Be A Good Example

"You may not be able to change the world with one smile, but you may be able to change one person's world with a smile."

~ Kate Sims

No matter who we are, what we do, our age, race or creed, we can lead by example.

Mahatma Gandhi inspired movements for civil rights and freedom across the world in several countries and was a perfect example that one person can change the world. We must be the change we want to see because change can ONLY begin with us. Good leaders know that telling others what to do is not as effective as living by the values you want others to follow.

Years ago, I heard a great expression that stuck with me and has served me well; "Always remember who you are, where you're at, and what you're doing."

Leading by example is incredibly effective. Whether we're recognized for our actions or not, being conscious of what we did and how we felt about it does wonders for our self and is nothing but good karma. Helping others and giving back is one of the most satisfying and rewarding things in the world. People are always looking for an example to follow, and being that example paves the way for others to become great as well.

Some of our most valuable life lessons we learn from our parents, mentors, and teachers. Having good examples when we are younger are important because they are the impressions that shape our values, attitudes and beliefs. We must be aware of our actions every day because they will affect the minds of others, which in turn will affect the future of our world.

Sometimes we are not even aware we are being an example, whether it is good or bad. I remember watching my uncle smoking and blowing smoke rings and wanting to be cool like him. Little or big, people are watching what we do, so we must try to watch what we say and do and be the person that you would like to follow. Do and say things, whether in private or public, that you know will put you on the right path towards success or bring good vibes to someone else's day.

I hope something in these chapters has inspired change in a positive way, not only for personal enrichment, but to see the value in giving back and paying it forward. If we all practice even just a little of this, our world will be on its feet in no time. Even if Covid-19 never existed, and when it becomes a part of our history, there will always be opportunities to learn and grow from. We will be able to get through anything, if we have the support of each other.

When we feel we are doing good things, contributing in a positive way, we will smile again.

The following are 5 powerful life changing lessons from Gandhi that we can learn to practice and lead by example:

#1: Change Yourself First
"Be the change you want to see in the world."
— Mahatma Gandhi

The concept of changing yourself to reflect what you want to see around you is simple in theory, but requires hard work, patience and determination to attain. Gandhi taught this important principle in his words but epitomized them in his actions. Even when facing imprisonment, hunger and possible death, Gandhi remained steadfast, loving, and peaceful.

Can we summon the strength of character to live the change we wish to see?

#2: Strength Through Peace

"There are many causes that I am prepared to die for but no cause that I am prepared to kill for."

— Mahatma Gandhi

Gandhi was a revolutionary, a hero, and the leader of a nation. He led his people to independence and self-rule through his extraordinary strength.

And... he did it without hurting anyone.

Such a concept today seems unfathomable and unattainable. Gandhi's achievements show otherwise. He showed that self-sacrifice and courage – not death and destruction – can produce change.

We have the capability to change the world through peaceful activism, demonstrating love, and living unselfishly. Let us do so.

#3: Violence is Unnecessary
"An eye for an eye will only make the whole world blind."
— Mahatma Gandhi

The only thing that Gandhi hated in his life was violence. There are more quotes and teachings about violence from Mahatma Gandhi than any other topic. Somewhere in the world, there is a conflict going on. Innocent lives are being lost, along with the lives of those fighting. Gandhi taught that our cultural, religious and political differences are no excuse to hurt, much less kill, anyone.

#4: Pursue the Truth
"Even if you are a minority of one, the truth is the truth."
— Mahatma Gandhi

Needless to say, Gandhi was a big proponent of truthfulness. He warned people against blindly accepting information without careful examination. Propaganda doesn't make something true. Repeating of information doesn't make something true. The attainment of truth happens through careful examination, a critical eye, and an open mind. Examine things for yourself. Our world will be a much better place when this becomes more common.

#5: Watch Your Thoughts

"A man is but the product of his thoughts. What he thinks, he becomes."

— Mahatma Gandhi

Gandhi was a man of incredible self-discipline and strength of will. The only way he was able to achieve what he did, despite sometimes horrendous treatment, was through conscious, productive, positive thinking.

Indeed, we are a product of our thoughts. Imagine a world of positive thinking and self-restraint. Gandhi did, and so can we. Gaining control of your thoughts and primarily thinking positive can transform your whole life. The more people who do, the better the world we live in will be.

Chapter Twenty-Nine
Good for the Soul

"A smile is happiness you'll find right under your nose."

~ Tom Wilson

I t's been said, "A picture is worth a thousand words," but maybe it should be, "A smile is worth a thousand words."

Have you ever had someone smile at you and it pierces through to warm your heart? A smile is powerful and the greatest universal connection of mankind. If love at first sight exists, it would be because of our smile. Eyes may be the windows to our souls, but the smile reaches our heart.

I see why Elvis Presley was the biggest sex symbol of our time. His voice captivated us, but his smile mesmerized us. He had the best smile ever! I love watching him in old movies and concerts just to see that beautiful smile light up the room.

Aside from eating healthy and exercise, smiling is one of the healthiest things we can do, and it's also therapy to make someone else smile. Studies show smiling releases feel good chemicals like endorphins and serotonin in our brain which makes us feel good. As well, those who smile a lot typically live longer healthier lives.

When we smile at someone, it coaxes them to smile back at us. Try it out to see if I'm right. Your smile alone has the power to make someone's day, so smile more!

Research also indicates that smiling makes us better looking and more attractive.

When I first became acquainted with ICU in Children's Hospital, I was a deer caught in headlights. All around me was sick babies and children on life support. I remember seeing parents and nurses smiling and laughing sometimes. I would think, 'What the hell is wrong with them? Their child is on the brink of death.'

After a few weeks, I occasionally noticed Cam and I laughing at something funny one of the nurses would say as we got to know them better. I began to understand why the other parents would have moments of reprieve and laughter. It was the only thing to keep them going on some days. I remember thinking how wonderful it was to smile again. I never realized how important it was until it was gone. That goes with a lot of things about life, like my grandma telling me how she never appreciated her leg for all its great purpose until it was gone. We learn from our own experiences, but one's from others can be just as mighty.

We love being around babies so much because they smile about four hundred times a day. Really happy adults smile about fifty times in a day, and the average being 20 times or less.

Let's smile more by trying to focus on positive happy thoughts. It's much easier to do when we know we can choose our thoughts. And since it's a choice, why not choose happy ones!

Smile Again

Chapter Thirty
Beauty is in the Eye of the Beholder

"Every time you smile at someone, it is an action of love, a gift to that person, a beautiful thing."

~ Mother Teresa

Another saying my grandma would always say, "You're only as beautiful on the outside as you are on the inside." Of course, when we are Ten, that makes no sense. I knew pretty people that weren't nice. But then as I aged, I started to notice that when I came to know someone, their looks would physically change. Average looking people became gorgeous, and some good-looking people became disenchanting. By George, my grandma was right again!

For any of my suggestions and recommendations in this book to make a positive impact, you will need to like yourself, believe in yourself and remind yourself every day. If you don't like yourself, any self-improvements will fall short. I have learned many interesting facts counseling people about self-image during my years as a medical aesthetic consultant.

People come to see me for advice on such things as acne scaring, sun damage, anti-aging treatments, among others. However, if they don't already love themselves, no treatment will replace that. They may feel better temporarily, but it isn't a fix all.

Quite often I ask patients if I'm correct when I say, "When you look in the mirror, you probably only zoom in to what you don't like whether it's wrinkles, scars, or a big nose, etc. You don't look at yourself and say, I have a great smile. I have nice eyes, or anything positive."

The patient usually nods and looks at me like I'm psychic or something. They agree that they never notice any of the good things. It's a powerful eye-opening realization, and some people cry once I point out their beautiful traits, including their personality.

There is nothing wrong with receiving treatments to compliment ourselves, once we know we are simply adding an enhancement to the terrific person we already are!

It's not that difficult to change our thought pattern once we realize we can. I probably should have called this book, *Awaken the Awareness in You*, because anything can be achieved when we become aware of what we want... aware that everything is a choice... and aware we choose our own thoughts!

We can all find some good in us, and each other when we choose to. Focusing on our faults is a choice, and a very bad habit that thankfully we can break! With concentration and practice, we can like ourselves more than we thought possible. There will always be things we don't like, but we don't have to give it our attention... switch gears and shift thoughts to better ones. It took me some time, but now I usually can change my thoughts as easy as flicking a light switch.

Try to say positive affirmations every day, multiple times a day! Again, this takes time to become effective and consistent. When I first started doing it, it didn't come naturally, and felt odd to say things like, 'everything always works out for me.' Probably because I didn't completely feel that way, but I kept persisting, and now I completely feel everything always works out for me. If something in my day doesn't go as expected, I know it's just a little bit of needed contrast.

Everybody can choose their own affirmations, and if you are not sure what that looks like, go online and research some affirmations that appeal to you. Depending on the day, mine sometimes change, but usually I start by saying a little personal prayer and follow by saying how grateful I am for whatever I am feeling that day. I ask the Universe to continue blessing me with feeling gratitude for all the wonderful things I receive. To help me say and do the right things and appreciate the lovely people in my life.

What seemed like an effort in the beginning is now one of my favorite daily things to look forward to.

Chapter Thirty-One
Persistence

"A smile is a curve that sets everything straight."

~ Phyllis Diller

I almost didn't add this chapter because throughout this book I talk about persistence, and its need for so many things in order to find success and satisfaction. However, because I believe it is one of the most valued traits, I will expand.

Time and time again, I see people just give up and quit too soon. But then, I see people who reach their goals and dreams because they were persistent. As you recall in earlier chapters, some of the most successful and happy people in life were those who had endurance. They never gave up because it simply wasn't an option.

Whether it is something small like countless attempts to thread a needle, or the numerous auditions to finally get cast in a Steven Spielberg movie, endurance is a quality that we need to succeed at, whatever our endeavors are.

I know a person who had always wanted to be a paramedic, and in her forties decided to take the course. I was so proud of her for following her dream. That's a tough training program and learning new things can be more challenging when we are older because the transmission of nerve impulses between cells slows down. (Exercise helps prevent this!)

It was one of the more difficult things she has done, and it took her three times before passing the course. Most... probably 99% would have given up on the first or second try, but not her. I have always loved and admired her, but after that, I had a newfound respect and think of her as one of the most resilient and determined people I know. And she is amazing at her job!

With persistence all the many things that didn't come easy for us, can eventually come with ease.

In my youth, I vividly recall walking the wooden fence all around our farm. The circumference in total must have been close to a half mile. Living in a rural area growing up in the seventies there wasn't a lot to do, so this was a good time killer, and exercise in patience. The objective was to walk all the way around without falling. If I fell, I would have to start in the beginning. Well, sometimes I would be almost all the way around, lose my balance and fall off. Some days I would be so frustrated and want to give up, but I never did. Only once did I stop before I finished was because it was getting dark out, and my mom made me come in. But you can imagine how much sweeter the reward after many futile attempts to finally make it. It felt like I won an Olympic medal!

When things come too easy, we sometimes don't appreciate it as much as we would if we put a lot of hard work in. We all love the underdog more than the easy achiever because they've had to work so much harder to reach their goal. Perhaps we root for the underdog because we know that they have much more tenacity because of their relentless determination and persistence.

Persistence pays off. Most great stories of success of any nature usually comes with a combination of confidence, faith and persistence, which I believe to be a magic formula.

Smile Again

Chapter 32
Be Kind

'Kindness is being someone who makes everyone feel like a somebody.'

~ RAKtivist

I thought the last chapter was the finish line, but I felt the need to add this one. It's important to acknowledge during and following this pandemic, kindness will be pivotal to get us through.

Can you imagine what our world would look like if everyone was kind? It makes me happy to think what that would look like, and all the harmony it would bring. But it also makes me feel sad because it seems like sometimes we are going in the opposite direction to make that happen. Violence, crime, racism, defamatory people, and many other factors are escalating and constricting harmony.

Our ego and pain-body promotes conflict and ill will. I hope my definition of these in my previous chapters provide a little bit of enlightenment to make being kind a little easier. Being unkind doesn't serve us or anybody, and only feeds the egoic mind.

People who like to read books like this one are usually ones who wish to improve, be inspired and uplifted to live a wonderful life. Sometimes we get caught in the 'hustle and bustle' of life, and unintentionally lose sight of what really matters. This is where a little reflecting comes in handy. As I mentioned earlier, we want to live in the present more often, and drudging up the past can be futile. However, at times our past can be a great learning tool.

Think back to a time when someone was very mean to you. How does that make you feel? Obviously not good. Now think of a time when someone was very kind to you. It probably brings a little smile. It's easy to be kind; all we have to do is be aware, and remind ourselves how our actions can affect others. Treat people the way you would like them to treat you. Agree to disagree. Let go of things you can't control. It's difficult, or even impossible to be kind if your brewing negativity. I can't repeat enough how our thoughts and behaviors are completely our choice to control.

I know that during this pandemic it requires more effort to be kind. Anxious tension and uncertainty can conflict with our natural state of normalcy, but this is when we need to step up our game. We are all affected from this Covid pandemic and it will linger for years. Please keep in mind, some people are more adversely affected than others. Many have and will have suffer devastating losses. Let's reach out to all in need.

I try to always think before I act. Typically our impulses drive us to judge before thinking. Do I really need to say something that may cause upset? Will there be any benefit? I may not have to be kind in every situation, but I don't have to be mean. Walking away can even be a kind gesture rather than ensuing in words of conflict.

Challenge yourself to be kind to someone who is being selfish or grumpy sometime. Don't judge; you don't know their story behind the face, and chances are it is a sad one, or they've had a really bad day. See if you can turn their frown upside down. It will probably be a very gratifying feeling if you can succeed.

Smile Again will provide some awareness and guidance to help cope with challenging times, see the silver linings that can come from adversity, and find more ways to live your best life. To be happy not only once you achieve your desires, but be happy along the way. When I started writing this book, I was excited and anticipating the finish line, but I reminded myself to live in the moment and enjoy the process of each chapter coming together with the wish to make a positive difference in a perilous time.

Smile Again

I hope you always find a reason to smile.

God Bless

Acknowledgements

It has been a pleasure to share my thoughts and knowledge gained through my experiences. As I mentioned in the beginning, I have been wanting to write **Smile Again** for many years. It seems that waiting all this time was a blessing in disguise. It was written exactly when our nation needed it most. Whether it's been a diversion, or informative, I hope you have become more aware of the possibilities to smile again.

Every day before I sat in front of my computer to write, I said a prayer to give strength and peace to all those who are suffering. I prayed for all of us to come together and help in any way we could. Even something as simple as staying home was saving lives. I prayed for this pandemic to end, and for us all to rebuild and restore. I asked the Universe to help me know the right things to say so I could make a positive impact in someone's life.

Thank you, Jesse. When I began to see this virus was going to become a threat to our livelihood, I was most worried about how you were going to deal with it all. I know how you are so social and love your outside life of volunteering and giving to others. The thought of you having to self-isolate at home for possibly months was going to be especially difficult. However, you surpassed all my expectations. I'm so proud or your courage and ability to make everyday a great one. Your eagerness to help with everything, and your company on our walks helped me find an appreciation for staying at home.

Thank you, Avery. You made self-isolating a good experience for me. Your maturity to deal with such a huge disruption in your life, made me proud. Stepping up with all your help and never complaining, further reiterated we raised a great son. We didn't even get into one squabble, and you kept so positive through it all.

Thank you, Cam. You made me feel everything was going to be okay and kept fear away from our door. You worked hard through this pandemic with bravery and never complained. You made it easy to stay at home.

Thank you to Mom. It was a comfort to be able to talk to you every day and have our social distant visits outside when I brought you your groceries. Shopping for you made me feel good. Having you here to buy groceries for elevated my gratitude.

Thank you to all the frontline, essential workers. You risked your lives every day to save lives, sacrificing your own life to save others. You are heroes and I hope we honor you in the ways that you deserve.

Thank you all my 'bubble' friends. You have been a comfort in an unstable time, and provided some normalcy surrounding much uncertainty. It's been wonderful to laugh and temporarily escape the unrest we are facing. Thank you Penelope for the beautiful painting for this book cover. It's very symbolic because I know we can rise through the cracks to *'smile again'.*

As I am finishing this book, we are in November 2020. Since I began writing, there has been much more devastation and loss. Our hopes were slightly when most countries started to 'flatten the curve', and begin re-opening. Unfortunately, Covid cases began to rise again, and face the second wave. I pray we have better tools and knowledge this time, so we don't see such drastic effects as earlier this year. I also pray for everyone to find some peace, solace and comfort to carry us through to brighter days.

.

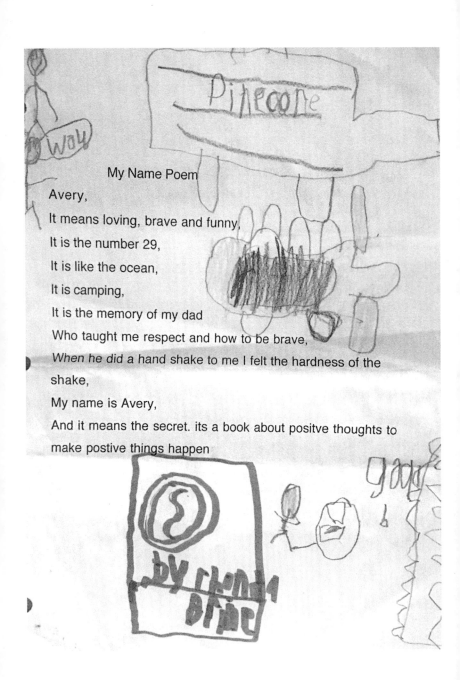

My Name Poem

Avery,

It means loving, brave and funny,

It is the number 29,

It is like the ocean,

It is camping,

It is the memory of my dad

Who taught me respect and how to be brave,

When he did a hand shake to me I felt the hardness of the shake,

My name is Avery,

And it means the secret. its a book about positve thoughts to make postive things happen